Werner Loos

God is Not Alone

The Dissolution of Evil:

A Practical and Philosophical Examination

Bibliographic information from the German National Library: The German National Library lists this publication German National Bibliography; detailed bibliographic data are available on the Internet at dnb.dnb.de.

Editing and proofreading:
Ursula Dimper, Margrit Wilhelmine Neidhardt

Published: BoD - Books on Demand GmbH,
In de Tarpen 42, 22848 Norderstedt, bod@bod.de
Printed by: Libri Plureos GmbH, Friedensallee 273,
22763 Hamburg
ISBN: 978-3-7693-9870-0

What is wrong with the people in the world?

Our present existence is hurtling toward a catastrophic future because of our harmful behaviors. The amount of damage to and destruction of our environment is growing and it appears to be unstoppable. Despite numerous warnings by scientists and protests organized by various groups, there has been no significant improvement in the behavior of those primarily responsible. This raises the following questions: What is the cause of this phenomenon? Why does suffering, sadness, and pain, but also love, exist in our world? Is there a God, and is He able and willing to help or not? What is the meaning of the tragedy that makes up our lives?

'A glimpse into the world proves that horror is nothing other than reality.'

(Alfred Hitchcock)

These questions have been troubling my mind for many years. Now, in this book, I have summarized and written down my findings.

My book delves into the world of the seemingly incomprehensible. It contains explanations and answers that have never been put down on paper before. It explains the reasons for our existence, our behavior, and how it will all end.

You, the reader, are given the opportunity to relate the findings and answers in this book to your own life experiences and to understand the meaning of your life.

My special thanks go to my editors and proofreaders

Ursula Dimper and Margrit Wilhelmine Neidhardt.
Their expertise made this book possible in its present form.

Munich, Germany, February 2025

Table of Contents

Preface

My mother's condition was getting worse by the day. The doctors said she had five months at most to live; her pancreatic cancer was incurable, and sometimes during my frequent visits it seemed to me that she was relieved that it was coming to an end. She didn't say so, but I could tell. For many years, her life had consisted of pain in her hip joints, walking was difficult, and she lived in constant strife with her husband, my father. And now this cancer. I could understand my mother wanting to 'go'. I often stood at her bedside in the hospital with other family members. On the day she died, she sat up with her eyes wide open, staring into space, despite her infirmities, only to fall back onto the sheets after a few seconds. Then I closed her eyes. Two years later, my father died of a heart attack, which made me very sad in spite of everything and the way he had treated my mother. Only many years later, looking back, did I realize that the death of my parents had been a kind of turning point in my emotional state. I was very interested in philosophy and its explanations of the world, human existence, and the existence of God. After years of studying these topics and the many different explanations, a new certainty about the causes and consequences of mundane existences seemed to have formed in my mind.

In researching my book, I noticed that scientific explanations of the topics of life, suffering, love, death, and many others are always descriptive. The reasons for their existence have never been conclusively explained to me.

For centuries, people have used logic and science to try to explain the world and its existence, but questions about what the human mind is, how to explain its consciousness and its thoughts, cannot be answered by the natural sciences. Neither do representatives of the Church have conclusive knowledge for me as to why the world and suffering exist. They say that this makes it all the more important to believe in God.

There are both proponents and opponents of certain theories about the existence of existence. So which side should I take? I am not criticizing this state of affairs in any way. It can be seen as bad or good. However, as I will describe later in this book, the situation is exactly as it should be. Many people wonder if God is doing anything about the coming crises, which may end catastrophically, and if He will help us, or if there is no God and everything is inevitable. Or if there is a God who cannot or chooses even not to help us.

As the planet's living conditions continue to deteriorate, more and more people are becoming aware of the dangers in their own lives and want to see changes in existing systems and in the behavior of those they hold responsible for the coming catastrophes in order to preserve Creation. At the same time, there are groups that want to safeguard their own wealth and prosperity.

At present, there are no answers to the question of the purpose of human action and suffering, whether there is any chance of improvement, or whether we are all doomed. There are people who imagine that all actions are predetermined. Living beings are born into the world, suffer and love until they die. Then the cycle starts all over again. That is the whole shebang, to put it simply. This concept dispenses with the need to ask questions, because everything is preordained. The question about God remains unanswered. Nor can it be answered, as I will explain later in the book. On the one hand, the existence of God is denied; on the other hand, there is belief in a God whose existence cannot be proven. For many people, their belief in God is linked to their hope for an end to the suffering. Interesting are the contradictory hypotheses that, on the one hand, there must be a creator who created everything, and that, on the other hand, everything came into being by chance.

My first inquiry deals primarily with the motive of why I want to know and ask various things. Not in the sense of a question that I need to ask in order to perform an action or function. Such questions are ones I ask because I do not know something and want to know it. This comes from curiosity, a character trait that is inherent to my subconscious and manifests itself in my behavior. I am not happy with this knowing that I am behaving unconsciously, but I have to accept it. What is nescience, and what influence does it have on me? Humanity (and with it nature) is in a state of flux, the end of which will be the dissolution of not all, but many forms of life. Not all living beings will die, and our planet will not become completely hostile to life. There will, however, be something of a new beginning with fewer of the negative character traits in evidence. In this book I explain and describe the reasons that have led to and are leading to this development. It is clear that we humans are the ones who manifest both negative character traits and love in our mundane existence. We will continue to do so until all existence inevitably dissolves. That is the reason why we and the world were created. The evil nature and love that exist in our nescient character traits bring all the suffering and all the love into this mundane existence, and God Himself exists in all living beings, so He is not an observer, but an instigator and participant.

With the knowledge I have gleaned, I can understand everything that is happening on our planet. It also provides me with all the answers to the questions I asked myself while I was writing this book. In this book, I describe how I arrived at my findings, why I am convinced of my conclusions, and how new questions and answers have been added in the course of my intensive study of these topics.

As with everything in life, nothing happens without a reason. I am not writing this book just for myself or because of myself. I am writing it because it might also help other people to see the reasons for their own behavior. If readers can engage with its contents, they may understand why there is suffering and love and where life is going. This may lead them to losing or at least to some extent allying their fear of the future and allow them to live in less suffering and with more awareness.

*'He who has a **why** to live for can bear almost any how.'*
(Friedrich Nietzsche)

Explanation of terms:

In this book, I use the word **bad** to mean the same as **evil**. I know that the word bad can also be used to refer to events that occur where there is no human influence, such as earthquakes, tsunamis, and droughts. I am of the opinion that the word 'evil' is often only used in connection with serious actions. Less serious actions, such as those curiosity or slothfulness of the mind, are not usually attributed to evil.

I would like to point out in particular that my explanations merely represent my understanding of God and the world. I do not wish to criticize anyone, I do not wish to have a negative influence on other people or circumstances, and I do not claim to have written a scientific work.

Quotations from other authors are in italics, while my own explanations are in normal print.

Chapter 1

The development of my theories requires a careful examination of relevant topics. Through this examination, my understanding of human existence and the nature of the world has grown significantly. Ultimately, many of my insights have emerged from this process.

'What do you do to make the world a little more peaceful and beautiful? - I take my medication.'

(Anon.)

Body and Mind

The Body

Bodies are systems that are limited in time and space that are materially diverse. A living human body is a self-regulating and self-renewing system with different life cycles. Among other things, a body regulates its own temperature, ensures that its blood does not become acidic, carries out healing processes independently, and converts the nutrition in ingests into energy. These special processes are not controlled by human consciousness or a human mind but are predefined and independently operating life functions that are obviously regulated by the brain.   If I consider the human body in isolation, without mind, consciousness, and unconsciousness, I notice that it cannot provide food and energy itself; it cannot not move on its own. All movements that facilitate the ingestion of food must therefore be initiated from an external source, that is, from an entity external to the physical body. The coordinated actions of muscles, tendons and bones that facilitate the acquisition, preparation and ingestion of food, as well as the acts of chewing and swallowing, are initiated by the human mind through the agency of the brain. The human mind does not move every single muscle, joint, tendon, or even cell. To illustrate this, consider the simple action of drinking a cup of coffee. If the mind tried to control every part of the body involved in this action, large or small, it would be overwhelmed. It would also have to constantly check that the parts of the body were moving in a purposeful way and adjust them if necessary. To do this, the mind would have to rapidly process the corresponding sensory signals, assess their alignment with goals, and confirm them or make adjustments as necessary. The brain does all this; it can do it better than my human mind ever could. The human brain was designed to do this, and it continues to evolve according to the purposes at hand. How the brain develops can be observed in an infant. An infant's body must be nourished and cared for by its parents or it will die. The infant's mind and brain cannot do this alone; they have not yet reached the appropriate stage of development. Only when they have developed enough can they take care of themselves. The very elderly experience a decline in physical condition

and their mobility is also reduced.

'As you get older, three things happen. The first is your memory goes, and I can't remember the other two.'.

(Sir Norman Wisdom)

As with an infant, an elderly person is nourished and assisted in movement by other people. However, unlike an infant, their mental faculties can still be high. The human body can be regarded as an independently functioning, fundamentally viable system. However, it requires an external force to initiate movement and sustain life.

The Human Mind

The human mind is a mundane mental entity attached to the mundane physical body. The concept of the mundane human mind is understood to include thought or consciousness, which will be described later in this book. This means that the human mind, made up of myself, is made up of thoughts. These thoughts are derived from information present in my brain that has been transmitted from a motivational unconscious mental sphere and from sensory perceptions in my brain. This transmitted information subsequently forms the constituent patterns and arrangements of the cells in my brain, which are then recorded and interpreted by my human mind as thoughts. At the behest of my mind, my brain translates my thoughts into physical activities, according to their content. The human senses appear to be perceived by the mind at the point of reception or origin. For example, an odor is perceived by the re captors in the nose, a taste by the tongue, a sound by the ear, and so on. But to me this only appears to be superficial. The human environment is full of signals for all the senses. As a result, any sound present at an appropriate volume and frequency can be perceived by the sense of hearing, in accordance with its intended function. The sounds are then transmitted as signals to the brain via nerve pathways. The same thing happens with the eye, the nose, the tongue, etc. The corresponding signals are transmitted to the brain. The brain serves as the central point of contact, collection, and storage of all the sensory signals of the human body. When the human mind accesses the sensory signals received by the brain, it recognizes the sensory organs or body parts from where the signal originates and can, for example, make the body to move to avoid potential dangers.

Therefore there must be a mapping of the signals to the body's original point of reception in the brain. Otherwise, the human mind would not be able to classify which signals are coming from the ear, the eye, the mouth, the finger, and so on. This means that there must be placeholders in the brain for the original physical receptors. Namely placeholders for acoustic, visual, and all other sensory receptors.

I use the term 'placeholder' here for a special arrangement of the brain cells involved, a pattern created in the brain area according to the information content. It can be concluded from this that the human mind does not directly access the actual sensory receptors such as the eyes, ears, tongue, etc., but rather their placeholders in the brain. Therefore, any sensory signal would have to be perceived by the human mind only after it has been transported to the placeholder in the brain and not directly at the physical receptor. If this is true, then even physical pain cannot be perceived by the human mind directly at the point of origin in the body, but only at the corresponding placeholder in the brain.

Example:

If I injure my hand slightly on the edge of a table, I feel the pain immediately, that is, after the time it takes for the nerves to transmit it to my brain. But if I am in a situation of danger, e.g. there is a fire in the room and I have to escape quickly, I will probably not feel any pain if I bruise my hand on the edge of the table while escaping from the room; I will perceive the pain later. From this I conclude that the body cannot feel pain on its own, but that pain is an interpretation of the human mind. The pain is only felt when the mind perceives the information contained in the brain. Everything that my physical senses can pick up from the environment is transported to my brain and stored. But the brain does not perceive and interpret the biochemical and electromagnetic information it contains on its own; the human mind does this. If one were to assume that the brain is precisely the place where images, smells, and sounds, etc. are located, then it is theoretically conceivable that these could be found as images, smells, or sounds when the brain is dissected or scanned.

But science has not yet been able to do this. The information in the brain is captured and interpreted by the human mind.

The information interpreted by my human mind manifests as my own individual thoughts and is accessible only to me and to no other human mind. Thus, each person has their own human mind that is theirs and theirs alone and that can be distinguished from the omnipresent divine mind by the mundane presence in each person, yet is still a part of it.

The brain is made up of different kinds of matter, and it is a fundamental tenet of materialism that matter of any kind cannot have spiritual ideas or create consciousness. The brain's memory consists of special arrangements of cells that represent specific information content, such as a picture, a spoken word or an odor. Each item of information the brain receives through the sensory organs (optical, acoustic, gustatory, olfactory or sensory) is represented by a specifically assigned cell pattern. This cell pattern is then recognized by the human mind, which interprets it and thus creates ideas about the physical material world in which it lives.

Chapter 2

My insights have formed over the years in small, sometimes arduous steps. I have constantly had to address the questions mentioned at the beginning of this book because they simply wouldn't let me go. Added to this was my confrontation with the different, sometimes contradictory views and justifications of various philosophers, theologians, and scientists. Their statements have me only inadequate answers. And despite the detail of their explanations, they still didn't seem to penetrate into the essential questions about God and the world. I couldn't sufficiently explain and justify my personal experiences and my own actions with these explanations. This made it necessary for me to go into every detail in my mind in order to be able to answer all questions conclusively by myself. I should also be able to verify these answers in my everyday life and in my dealings with other people.

Fundamental Considerations and Answers

Is there a God?

'The word God is for me nothing more than the expression and product of human weaknesses, the Bible a collection of honorable, but still primitive legends' (Albert Einstein)

According to the Big Bang theory *(Georges Lemaître)*, the universe must have had a beginning. Science observes that it expands, and anything that expands must have had a beginning. It must have come into being at some point. The question of what was before the Big Bang cannot be answered because there is no evidence to indicate the existence of anything before the Big Bang. The universe and life can therefore not have arisen by chance. Nothing existed that could have created such a complex world and life by chance. I therefore believe it is very likely that the world and life were created by a Creator and did not occur by chance.

Evidence for the existence of God has not yet been found. Nor can it be found, not in the sense of a mundane existence; after all, God is not material. However, the assumption that there is a God, a Creator of this mundane existence and of all being, is well-founded.

There are several observations about this on *YouTube*.

Chance

We speak of chance when no causal explanation can be given for a single event or the coincidence of several events. When we seek to explain why things happen, we usually look for natural laws or the intentions of those involved. Giving 'chance' as an explanation is therefore signifies a renunciation of a causal explanation.

(Source: Wikipedia)

If humans cannot give a causal explanation for an event, this does not necessarily mean that there is no cause for it. The inexplicability is due to a lack of information about the cause and conditions of the event and a lack of human understanding. An event cannot take place without a cause. For an event to happen at all, there has to be something that exists in the first place, something that allows the event to occur. When a particular event occurs, it also presupposes certain conditions without which such an event cannot occur. When we talk about chance, we are merely showing the limitations of the human mind, which is incapable of explaining certain events and circumstances. In a game of dice, for example, it is assumed that when a dice with the numbers 1-6 is thrown, it is impossible to predict which number will be rolled. If a number is predicted and it is actually thrown, we call it chance. There is no way to explain how this number came to be thrown. However, there must have been conditions that led to exactly that number being thrown, otherwise it would not have been that number that came up, but another.

The conditions for the number thrown lie in the shape and nature of the dice, in the ambient environment, in the hand doing the throwing, and in other accompanying circumstances. Under these uniquely given, because constantly changing, constellations and conditions, only this one result was possible. The human mind cannot grasp such complex relationships because no human being can be omniscient. The conditions themselves cannot be permanent, because the circumstances are constantly changing, and nothing can be permanent. Therefore, if you try to understand, repeat, or comprehend all past events, you can only consider them from a theoretical past, from a conceptual construct. The conditions that existed at the time the die was thrown cannot be understood because they were not fully known to man. After that, they have changed irrevocably. The conditions of such events can neither be fully understood nor fully reconstructed. Scientifically speaking, at best, approximations can be made for a small fraction of the conditions. Chance is thus a word to explain events, circumstances, and conditions that cannot be completely captured by man. However, they must be present for something to happen by 'chance'.

So if we assume that our world and our lives came into existence by chance, then something must have existed that made this chance possible. The question that then arises is where the conditions for this chance came from, which is a scientifically unsolvable and unanswerable question.

Duality

Religious dualism is a worldview that originated in the first millennium BC. It can be found in East and South Asia as well as in Western Asia and the Western world. In the dualistic worldview, reality consists of two spheres that are absolutely opposed to each other. Not only are there two worlds, but there are also two eternal deities as creators who created these worlds. An invisible, spiritual world stands in contrast to the visible, material world. A world of light is often distinguished from a world of dark. The invisible spiritual world is the creation of a good God, while the material world is the work of an evil God.

(Source: Wikipedia)

I believe that there cannot be two gods who are equal. Two such gods would constantly strive to gain the upper hand over the other. Two equal gods also raise the insoluble question of their origin and the question of their creator, a question that could be asked ad infinitum. The statement about religious dualism, that there are two equal gods, does postulate the existence of evil, yet I do not find equating it with a god conclusive. My inherent belief is that evil must be present in God Himself. It cannot be external to Him, otherwise it would be impossible to formulate explanations about mundane existences.

The following section will clarify the question of why God would have created life, the world, and man.

If there is a Creator called God, then nothing can be separate from or external to Him, for that would again create a cycle of questions about origin, whereby the idea of internal or external to God cannot be explained from the material mundane being. No one in mundane existence can know and describe God, nor are there any descriptions of a place where God would be. There cannot be a space where the Creator resides. Who would have created that space? If there is no space where the Creator resides, then there can only be a space within the Creator. Thus a creation only be formed within the Creator. If it is true that there is nothing external to the Creator, then what is within me is also within God, or rather, first within God and then within me, because it has been transferred from Him into my mundane mind.

So when I laugh, the motive for it must first be present within God, and then it appears within my thoughts. God Himself will not be able to laugh, because nothing, no receptacle exists within which He could express Himself. Yet through my body, laughter can be expressed within the mundane being. This means that my inner spiritual state is a reflection of the divine inner being, or rather a part of it. Now I am experiencing in my life exactly what is within me. I am experiencing elements of the seven negative character traits and elements of love. When I consider my past, I can also see this in my actions at that time. Since God created me and brought me to life, these character traits that I believe are mine must first be present within God, otherwise I could not harbor them and experience them within me.

From this position, without wanting to appear arrogant or even megalomaniacal, I dare to attempt to take God's perspective. From His (my) point of view, evil is within Him. The negative character traits to be found in evil cannot live themselves out in God Himself, they have no way of doing so. So what can He do? The solution is to develop a creation in which evil can be experienced and acted out, and that is namely our world. God does not develop this creation because of a - to Him inherent - negative character trait, but out of His unconditional love. His motive is to allow evil to be experienced, not to dissolve evil.

The dissolution of evil is a consequence of experiencing it, not an intention of God's love.

How could God have created the world or even anything at all? It is impossible to create something eternal, permanent. To do so, there would have to be a beginning for what is to be created, something that was not there before. Can something unique be created? That is impossible as well, because if nothing exists, what can it be created from? So if something is to be created, it can only be something dual, the one side and its antithesis, something that cancels itself out and dissolves in the sum. This combination of created duality does not really exist as something permanently created, but as something transient that already contains the element of dissolution within it.   Thus duality forms the basis for the development of life. Since evil must already be present within God, it needs a world in which to act itself out. For this to occur, the

26

conditions need to be created in which the negative character traits can be experienced. However, it takes more than a mundane

material being, for evil could not experience itself in the world alone. Therefore, an antithesis has to be added to the evil that is to be experienced in the created world. Something that allows evil to be experienced: this something is love. Love brings its qualities as thoughts into the human brain. It brings about human actions that allow the never character traits to be fulfilled. A murderer needs a victim. A person who is hungry for power subjects to submit to his power. This is not only true from the point of view of a statesman. Power is also exercised in human relationships. Greedy people need others to satisfy their greed, for example, as enablers for their exploitation. For this purpose, love unconsciously enters into the corresponding human mind.

However, not everyone harbors 100% evil or 100% love within them for perfection cannot exist. Therefore, the distribution of evil and love always varies. A murderer's motive to take life is very strong. But as a family man, they may also take loving care of their children. In the mundane mind of a butcher, who kills countless animals throughout his working life, there is also an element part of love present when, for example, he comes home to his wife and helps her with the housework because she needs his help. Conversely, a loving person also has some negative character traits. In duality, both always have to be present. I use the term nescience to summarize evil and love.

What is love?

Love is the antithesis of evil, and its existence is a necessary consequence of a dualistic creation within our mundane being. Without love, evil could not experience itself. Therefore, love cannot exist for its own sake, nor can it stand alone.

Love enables, permits and suffers evil.

'Whenever you find yourself drawn into the drama of others, repeat these words: Not my circus, not my monkeys.' (Polish proverb)

But resisting the call of the nescience is not as easy as the proverb suggests. Human beings are not independent beings capable of making truly free choices. For example, if evil in the form of a human being wants to indulge its lust, love will offer a victim. It will enter into the human spirit of another person and allow evil to satisfy its desires. In such a case, the act of love is unconscious, for no one would deliberately and consciously offer themselves to a perpetrator to be violated or killed.

In a relationship where two people claim to love each other, the strength of their love reflects the degree to which they support each other. The more intensely one partner strives to fulfill the wishes of the other, the stronger and more unconditional their love becomes. Consequently, the intensity of one partner's negative traits is likely to be proportional to the intensity of the other partner's love. This means that even in the face of one partner's negative character traits, such as jealousy, lust for power, greed and similar, the other partner remains committed out of love. Love means suffering to fulfill the needs of evil, for it always serves to enable the experience of the negative traits of evil. With growing awareness, one may come to understand that the suffering of human beings and other living beings allows evil to manifest according to God's will.

What is right and what is wrong?

The discussion above makes it clear to me that there can be nothing that is wrong. Everything that happens in mundane existence must be right. These happenings are manifestations of evil and its antithesis, love; nothing else exists. Nevertheless, what happens is caused by something bad, it originally harbors evil (the bad) within itself. This leads to suffering, pain and sorrow, but also to devotion and love. Perhaps love, happiness and contentment are feelings of spiritual fulfillment. A form of satisfaction on the one side with the evil that was able to experience itself along with its motives, and on the other with the love that made it possible.

What is life?

Living things differ from the dead or immobile, such as a stone, in that they are alive. Not in the sense of movement, because a robot can move too, but in the sense of independent, spiritually willed movement of a physical, viable system. Life can only exist because there is a Creator of that life. Only God can create a living, self-regulating system out of matter. The body becomes alive when the Creator sets it into motion. This applies to all forms of life, including plants and animals. Every living being needs another living being as food in order to continue to survive. It cannot sustain itself with stones or sand. At the beginning of life, there was nothing in the world but the three elements of earth, water and air.

So the first living being had to be able to feed off or sustain itself from these elements. Plants were the first living organism. It was only through their existence that other living beings could be created, which could then use these plants as food. In this way, the capabilities of living beings that came afterward developed in such a way that other living beings could also serve as food. The Creator must have foreseen in this the capabilities for the physical development of man. I recognize this from the fact that the physical capabilities of human beings have evolved alongside the evolution of the primitive character traits. This means that the more advanced character traits of the nescience can also be experienced. This insight explains to me the concept of evolution: it is the ability, instilled into the human body by the Creator, to develop from simpler to more complex structures. The characteristics of the nescience can be experienced accordingly. In this way, the more primitive character traits can be experienced first. As these traits are acted out and weakened, the human body and brain develop further to allow the experiencing of more complex character traits. For example, this is how humans developed the ability to walk upright.

Before the creation of life, God created the conditions for life by creating the universe, the world and all physical laws. By the creation of life, I mean the beginning of mundane life, the birth of a living being, and especially the birth of a human being. Evil is the motive for the creation of living bodies. That allows evil to enter into mundane existence. Only in evil is there the need to form a unity living with bodies in order to act out all the motives contained within them in a mundane manner. When evil seeks to form a new living body to act out certain motives, a man and a woman are brought together. Love, which is part of the nescience, can play an important part in this. It can aid in the conception of a child in one or both partners, even if the physical and psychological conditions are not favorable. Conceived by this couple and given birth to by the mother, this person's behavior and development are shaped by the nescience (evil and love). Everything that is in it will sooner or later be experienced in a mundane way by people with these character traits. Here, every type of upbringing and influence forms elements of the character traits and elements of the unconscious. These character traits transfer thoughts into the brains of people in order to be experienced and acted out.

What is sin?

Sins arise from actions rooted in the seven negative character traits; they always arise from the nescience. Whatever happens is always related to evil and its negative character traits. Fundamentally, this is something that constitutes a perpetrator, but also corresponds to a victim out of love. Both exist in varying degrees in the mundane world and are thus experienced by human beings.

The term 'sin' probably represents something bad to most people, and sinful actions are also punished. However, the avoidance of sin stops evil being experienced in order to ultimately end in self dissolution. Sinful actions performed by children, such as stealing, insulting, and hurting others, lead to sinful actions performed by parents, such as anger, revenge, and retaliation. Sin cannot actually be avoided because human beings are not beings capable of making choices of their own free will. The matter is always one of experiencing character traits.

What is good?

Good is generally considered to be the antithesis of evil. Modern philosophy suggests that an action is good if it serves life. However, judgment becomes difficult when it comes to the matter of a hero. A heroic act is meant to protect people from evil. But a hero who wants to protect other lives must also resort to evil deeds. The hero must force people with negative character traits not to carry out their actions. A hero will even have to kill people in armed conflicts to protect the lives of his comrades. Therefore, the good in a hero is only one element of love, whose motive is to protect the life of one or more people. However, love is also coupled with the negative characters qualities of evil, which the hero uses to harm or kill other people or life forms. It is therefore difficult to classify a hero as fundamentally good. When a person helps another, at first sight it appears fundamentally good. But one also consider what from the help takes and why it is given. The person being helped is in a situation of disadvantage. For example, he hit his girlfriend out of jealousy, so she wants to report him to the police. The intention behind the help here is to protect him from the consequences. He turns to a friend for help. Is the help the friend gives a good thing?? From the perpetrator's point of view, it is, but not for his battered girlfriend. And does it correspond to the general concept of good? For example, if poor, starving children are helped with food, is that not a good thing? But why are these children poor and hungry? They were conceived without any prospect of food security. Who would do such a thing? The reason lies in the negative character traits of the parents. Every child born of a relationship will also have to experience purposes that arise from the nescience So some good is made up of an element that is love and an element that us evil. It all depends on the experience of evil. Evil performs wrong actions with good intentions. Love is the antithesis of evil and was created as a necessity to do evil in the world.

Two apt quotes from Goethe on this subject:

'Two souls, alas, are dwelling in my breast...'

'...I am a part of the power which eternally wills evil and eternally works good.'

Can man choose freely?

Human beings are defined by their bodies and their mundane minds.

All the actions and corresponding thoughts of every human being are brought into the world by the qualities of the nescience. In their mundane minds, people can only consciously recognize these qualities when they are sufficiently weakened. To judge whether a person is conscious or unconscious, we can distinguish between two possibilities.

First possibility:

The negative character traits are so strong that the human mind cannot consciously recognize them. Therefore, they will be fatefully, unconsciously, and unwaveringly translated into human action.

Second possibility:

A person who receives negative impulses from his subconscious mind will no longer put them into action when the traits have been severely weakened and are already predominantly acted out. This person can consciously recognize the negative thoughts present in his brain before he acts on them. In this case, they no longer react with spontaneous unconscious behavior to such thoughts. By consciously recognizing their negative thoughts, they can refuse to act on them. However, this ability does not make them free. This person receives messages from other, more subtle traits of their nescience. These, in turn, are so strong that they cannot consciously recognize them, and they must act them out in mundane actions to experience them. I believe that human beings are neither free nor can they choose the way they live. All appeals from humans to other humans to change (improve) their lives are of no relevance to humans in the first possibility mentioned above. They are so strongly bound to their negative character traits that they cannot deviate from them. Nevertheless, there is freedom, but in the sense that God has given evil the freedom to experience itself entirely according to its needs in the world created by God. For evil it is not subject to any rules or restrictions.

'Would you like veal or pork?'
'You know,' says the guest, 'I'm a neurobiologist, I don't believe in free will. I'll just wait to see what I order'. (Anon.)

Time

What exactly is time? Does time pass or is there something more to it? What can pass is what exists, and that is all living things with their mundane spirit and all seemingly immovable material things. It is this mundane existence that I can observe, and all existence is finite. Time does not exist in nature; it is a human construct. It divides the process of becoming and passing away into continuous phases. Therefore, it is not time that passes, but the living and material mundane existence mentioned above. The course of experiencing and dissolution is merely classified and indicated by the incremental (temporal) markers created by man, but man neither creates nor changes it. However, such a division of becoming and passing away cannot fully capture the process, since every temporal phase, however small, contains an interval that is not captured. This can be seen, for example, in the process of aging. Age is measured in years, and at exactly 1 second past midnight, you are one year older. But you age steadily over the course of your life, not abruptly after one year. This continuous change cannot be represented, not even with the second-by-second display on a clock.

A crucial realization is that everything that happens is irreversible and unrepeatable, because everything is in a constant state of flux and dissolution. Even timepieces themselves are affected by this. It follows from this that what I can perceive is always the past, therefore something that has already happened. I cannot see into the future or perceive what is happening now; for me to do that, it has to have already happened. For example, I can only perceive that a car accident has taken place after it has happened; I cannot perceive it beforehand or at the moment of the event. In this context, I refer to this perception as the act of perceiving through my senses. This means that, firstly, it takes time for the image of the car to reach my eye and, secondly, it takes time for the information to travel from my eye to my brain. Furthermore, everything in life is subject to change and dissolution, so what has happened must have changed before the information reaches my mind. This is made particularly clear when we consider our observation of the universe. The best telescopes in the world first capture an event that is light years away when the light carrying the information has traveled the distance back to Earth. By then, the event has already changed. They cannot be seen at the time the event happens because the light has not yet transmitted the information about the change to Earth. And even my thoughts, as a mundane mind, I can only perceive when they are in my brain. So it seems that the human mind can only perceive the past, but not the present.

Examples of Duality

A minority of humanity holds and exercises enormous power. This starts with industrialists who produce their products by exploiting human and natural resources. This also includes politicians whose thirst for power and greed leads them into corruption and the strategic elimination of competitors. Once they have achieved their goal and gained power, they work to consolidate and expand it. They disregard or pay little attention to the well-being of the people who elected them (in a democracy). In a dictatorship, on the other hand, conditions are created by force, and the oppressed are silenced and forced into certain behaviors by the threat of further violence.

The counter-movement to these conditions consists of people who want to bring about change through demonstrations and other means of influence. These people are concerned with creating a better world where everyone lives together in peace.

Power is exercised in human relationships where people are dependent on and oppressed by one or more people in that relationship. These oppressed individuals cannot escape and are forced to suffer because their dependence on the oppressor is too strong. This allows the oppressor's negative character traits to manifest. It is unrealistic to believe that the better world desired can be built. The motive to develop a peaceful coexistence between all life forms is missing. What purpose would that serve? How would the lives of all the creatures of the earth function in an imaginary paradise? Firth, there would be no more killing. No living being would have to kill another living being in order to survive. This consideration alone leads to the assumption that this would lead to some kind of perfection. However, in my later deliberations on perfection, I will explain why this is not possible. Every person must grapple with their evolving beliefs, their life story, and the environment in which they live. In the same way, they must deal with the opposing or at least different beliefs of other people. These beliefs are the presets from the nescience that are inserted into the human brain. People are afraid of suffering. They are made to suffer by other people, by the environment, even themselves. That is why there is a division into good and evil, and it is always the other people who are evil, while oneself is the victim.

A perpetrator does not whine; they do not seem to be afraid of suffering. They simply act. They harm, destroy, and spread fear. Therefore, perpetrators are the evil ones, and other people do not want to have anything to do with these evil people. They are rejected, imprisoned, or even killed.

A victim thinks only of their personal suffering. They inevitably and fatefully see themselves as miserable losers who must submit to their suffering without being able to do anything about it. They seldom consider whether they are not themselves perpetrators, for example against animals and plants, and other people, or perhaps even in a subtle way against their own bodies.

The powerful do not want to give up their power, they want to satisfy their needs with all their might. They want to oppress more people, have more influence and increase their power. They want to rule the whole world and be unchallengeable. The oppressed want to end the suffering inflicted upon them by the powerful. They want to reduce the power of the powerful, by force if necessary. The oppressed are not alone. There are more oppressed people than there are powerful. Unlike the powerful, the oppressed seek what unites them, what makes them equal. They are united in their common suffering and unite against the powerful. They overthrow the powerful who oppress them by force. Now they are in power, and from their ranks new powerful people emerge. When a person does something, their body acts, moved by the nescient character traits that they are experiencing. So there is always a motive rooted in evil and a motive rooted in love behind every physical human action. Physical action is the only way for all the character traits to experience themselves in mundane existence. Therefore, these character traits cannot be restricted or prevented from being experienced. After all, mundane existence was created by the Creator for this purpose. Only when the worst character traits have sufficiently weakened can the next, more subtle ones be experienced in mundane existence. For example, the killing of human or living beings is followed by the manipulation of human and living beings, and so forth. For this to happen, the human body, including the brain, has to evolve. The mundane body with the brain of a native of the island of Borneo, for example, would not, by way of example, be capable of thinking about the production of artificial intelligence. Their body and brain are trained to express primitive character traits, such as the exercise of power within his tribe. Every product manufacturer fundamentally faces a problem that will arise, at least in the medium term.

The problem for the producer is, on the one hand, that they have to manufacture a high-quality and durable product so that it can be sold as often as possible from a qualitative point of view, but on the other hand, the sale of this product is finite. So, if there are no more people who want to buy this product because they already own it and will not need to buy another one in the foreseeable future due to its quality and durability, then its production would have to be discontinued. The manufacturer will therefore be tempted to compromise between product quality and durability in order to ensure sales for as long as possible. For example, they may equip his product with a component that will fail after a certain period of time making it necessary for a new product to be ordered. They may also take other measures to ensure that production and sales continue. Moreover, every company strategy is focused on survival, profitability, and growth. Power and greed are exercised as central motives in the character of these strategists and cannot be influenced until the nescient character traits of evil have sufficiently weakened. Most people, at least in Western democracies, want to achieve as much prosperity as possible and, once they have achieved it, never give it up again. In the process, several unconscious character traits come to the fore. These include stinginess, selfishness and greed. The problem for people in poor countries is that their governments enrich themselves at their expense and at the expense of their country. This leads to a scarcity of food and jobs, and they will soon lack the basic necessities of life. It is thus conceivable that there will be an increasing global migration of people to countries that can offer them better living conditions.

Because these people are fleeing for their lives, it is impossible to stop immigration, at least in democracies. Most philosophers and theologians speak of an impending catastrophe that will likely be unavoidable. Although many people recognize this, they can do nothing about it. They are not in a position to push through decisive improvements. It is becoming increasingly clear that, due to the aforementioned deteriorating conditions and ongoing conflicts over the remaining resources, the majority of people (and many other living beings) will no longer be able to survive in the future and will therefore perish. The few who survive will start afresh, bringing different character traits into the world and experiencing them. Humanity will not die out and the world will not perish, but there will likely be a new beginning for all life.

The Meaning of Life

The meaning of life is recognizable, it is not hidden. However, it can only be recognized by those people whose nescience has been relatively far outlived.

'The meaning of life is something that nobody knows exactly. In any case, it is of little use being the richest man in the graveyard.'
(Sir Peter Ustinov)

'The meaning of life is what you make of it.'

(Stephen Hawking)

The meaning of life is not to achieve a paradisaical state, for what purpose would that serve? Nor is it to be happy. Nor is it to believe that the meaning is hidden and that you can search for it and perhaps find it. Nor is it to do as much good as possible and nothing bad, in order to be somehow a more satisfied person. No, the meaning of life is in everything that we do. The reason why we live is revealed in all our actions and behaviors. Every questioner, every doubter, every person with firm convictions, every conspiracy theorist, but also every murderer, every thief and every criminal, every religious fanatic and every free spirit shows the meaning of their life in the way they live. For everything that exists within them emanates from evil and its antithesis, love, and it needs human bodies and the human mind so that evil and love can experience themselves in the world created by God. All living beings were and are born to this end.

Truth, an illusion?

The idea of restricting truth-bearing propositions to certain subject areas, such as those accessible to experience, is controversial. The precise determination of the objects to which this property is ascribed is equally controversial.

(the 'truth-bearers': judgments, beliefs, statements, contents, etc.). But the nature of truth as a property of truth-bearers is also a matter of debate (e.g., correspondence to 'truth-bearers', i.e., objects, states of affairs, etc., or 'coherence' as agreement with other truth-bearers). It is also controversial how we obtain

knowledge of this property: only through empirical knowledge ac-
quisition or, at least for certain objects, also in advance, 'a priori'.
(Source: Wikipedia)

Every observation and description of an existence in mundane existence is related to the conception of that existence in the individual human mind. No existence can be observed and described
without reference to the spiritual observer, because it is not possible to place oneself as a mundane spirit outside oneself in order to
observe an existence 'from the outside', so to speak. This means
that any existence can only be described and explained by analogy
with the concept of that existence formed in the human mind. In
addition, language is a form of expression and description that
obeys certain rules and preconditions, and therefore there can only
be verbal representations that correspond to these rules and preconditions. Thus no truth can be asserted about objective existence alone, because the description always correlates with the
conception of the human mind, and different human minds have
different conceptions, leading to different statements about the
perceived existence.

On the other hand, truth can be defined as follows and must be
able to fulfill the following criteria: Only that which is not subject to
change or impermanence can be true. Therefore, only that which
is eternal, absolute and unchanging can be true. These premises
also apply to perfection, so truth and perfection must be one. Every
known and imaginable existence in mundane existence is in constant flux because it is neither eternal nor perfect. A supposed description of a present state cannot be accurate, because the state

is already changing into another state while it is being described. There can be no state that remains even for a moment, because everything is in constant, uninterrupted flux. Moreover, every item of information is subject to constant change on its way to the recipient, so that what is perceived now cannot correspond to the original. There can be nothing original in the sense of something permanent because of constant experiencing and dissolution. Therefore, it is not possible to find or determine any evidence of natural existence in mundane existence. There is nothing in nature and in life that the human mind can observe or touch with its body that is demonstrable in the process. Demonstrable means that a repeatable process produces the same result or experience each time it is repeated. This is impossible because of the ever-changing nature of being. Everything is in a constant state of flux and is striving towards dissolution

Therefore, neither allegedly repeated experiments nor other repeated processes can:

a) have the same conditions. Nor can they be created as they were at the time of the first event or experiment to be repeated, because very few conditions are known.

b) produce the same result.

Of course, one could argue that mathematical results are true and therefore provable: $2 + 2 = 4$. But these are merely theoretical considerations, logical in themselves. But they do not occur in nature. If you substitute a natural existence for the numbers, you get the same problem as described above: For example, two apples +

two apples equals four apples: this is logical, but not provable, because each apple changes and is therefore not the same as before. The presence of four apples at that very moment depends only on the time frame in which the observation took place. After a certain time, they are no longer there because they have rotted and disintegrated. Physical laws are describable and measurable dependencies of a transient world. They regulate the behavior of systems and material beings among themselves. With the dissolution of matter, these laws also dissolve because there is nothing left on which they can act. Nevertheless, all ideas and opinions about provability and repeatability, including those from scientists, are exactly right. Their character traits, such as curiosity, vanity, self-righteousness, and need for power, also arise from the nescience and therefore try to play themselves out to the full. An interesting phenomenon is that although I speak of the need to be contained in God because there can be nothing external to Him, there is no clear term for this assumed truth. I can always speak either only of God or only of myself, although we are one, and even the word **we** consist of a duality. And when I speak of Him, I have to distinguish again, namely through the words **about Him** and the words about me. Even if I were to speak of **us**, a separate consideration has already occurred, because **we** describe at least two contents. So this supposed truth cannot even be expressed. The reason for this is duality and because of duality there can be no truth. However, I cannot say more about God than what my nescience has transmitted to my human mind and what I have experienced in my life and is present in my brain as stored information.

Perception and Interpretation

The human mind can only perceive what has already happened, not what is happening or will happen in the future. This seemingly trivial statement makes it clear that only the past, what has already happened, can be observed. We can only perceive those mundane phenomena that have already occurred, namely exclusively past events.

This applies not only to physical processes, but also to thoughts. When I think and act, I, as a human mind, can only observe (perceive) both after they have happened. Actions and thoughts belong to the past. That is why the human mind can only perceive and observe them after their mundane appearance, not immediately before or during their genesis. Only when thoughts are in the human brain, and only when an action has been performed, can the human, mundane mind perceive them.

I recently read an interesting article by Daniel Wegner, a psychologist at Harvard University in Boston.

In it he explains that,

'The fact that we have the experience of having willed an action does not prove that the will itself caused that action'. As early as the 1980s, American neurologist Benjamin Libet conducted a now-legendary experiment to investigate the link between thought and action. He asked subjects to decide whether they were going to bend a finger at a freely chosen moment. At the same time, he used electronic equipment to monitor the subjects' brain activity. The astonishing result: The motor areas in the

cerebral cortex became active a third to half a second earlier, even before the decision to bend the finger entered the subject's consciousness. In other words, the decision to act is made at an unconscious level before we consciously decide to do so.

So my human mind can therefore not be the one that is sending thoughts into my brain. There has to be another level of mind, and that is, as I said, the nescient mind. It sends impulses to my brain that my human mind can then recognize as its own thoughts. This then prompts my behavior in this mundane existence. I am the observer of my own behavior and of the information that constantly flows to me from other people, from my environment, or from the media. I notice that information affects me in different ways. I see that I - like apparently every human being - interpret and evaluate the information that comes to me differently. It seems impossible not to evaluate and interpret. Every interpretation of other people's behavior and of one's own behavior, as well as of processes or phenomena, is based on the ability of one's senses to register, but also on personal conditioning, i.e. the value base of the respective human mind that interprets and evaluates. My own actions, my own words, as well as my facial expressions and gestures are reflected by other people who observe me. Messages are sent back to me by the people who are affected or observing me after they have interpreted my actions. It turns out that I interpret my actions differently than do other people. Thus, there are different values underlying the respective interpretations.

If many people's senses (with the same sensory health) register the same events, such as during a visit to the theater, then subsequent questioning about their memories of the play and their evaluation of it would result in different perceptions and statements. These statements do not correspond fully or factually to the signals the senses received and which are present in the brain, but are based on the conditioning of the human mind. Thus, a critic will evaluate the play differently than a fan of the lead actor, and the author will describe his work as very successful, while some theater-goers may be a little disappointed by the production. Even with different interpretations, it must be assumed that the senses belonging to the critic, the fan, the author, or the audience member who experienced the play together perceived the same thing, provided that their senses functioned in approximately the same way. Just as their eyes must have transmitted all the light reflected by the event (the location is negligible) to the brain, all the other senses also received the corresponding signals and transmitted them to the brain If different parts of the total number of signals present in the brains of the audience members are selected and interpreted differently, then there must also be different conditioning of the respective human minds. Conditioning can be understood as a value potential that forms the basis for the selection, evaluation and assessment of what is perceived.

Perception and interpretation are therefore functions of the individual human mind, which selects from the totality of sensually recorded signals according to its conditioning. By conditioning I mean the characteristics of the nescience that are transmitted to the human brain that are present but ate different in each human brain. What is perceived also depends on the ranking of existing needs, where the strongest need has be satisfied first. For example, with hunger, the physical signals are present in the brain so that the human mind can react accordingly until the hunger is satisfied and the intake of food can be halted. You can, of course, also carry on eating and drinking. But because the body has already signaled it is satiated, this cannot be caused by signals from the body. What is more, there is now another need, a motive, to consume more food than the body requires. This motive is present again as an unconscious thought in the human brain. The human mind allows the body to act accordingly, hence satisfying the character traits that represent gluttony and excess. As described, the human mind is only capable of considering the past, but not the present or the future. Similarly, I can only consider my thoughts after they have appeared in my brain, namely after they have been transferred from the unconscious level to my brain. This view of the past is therefore the only one possible for the con-scious human mind.

The implication of this is that human action is not the result of a conscious human mind, for how can a human mind act consciously if it can only consider the past and its thoughts also represent the past?

Example:

When a person has a strong need for rest and sleep, the corresponding signals of this physical state are present in the brain. They human mind recognizes these signals and can occasion the body to rest. During sleep, the sensory organs (except the eyes) continue to receive signals and transmit them to the brain, because an interruption in the reception and signaling pathways is not associated with sleep, as the sensory organs are not, so-to-say, switched off. Only the mundane human mind seems to be absent, and so the human mind can no longer pick up signals received from the sensory organs. Quiet music or faint, distant sounds will not wake the sleeping person. However, if the signals are unfamiliar or the body is, for example, shaken violently, the human mind becomes active again, triggered by its nescience to ward off danger.

Another interesting observation is this:

There are people who are aroused from sleep even though they still need to sleep and they have not received any signals from the physical senses. The bedroom is quiet, there are no unusual smells or touches, and no sounds can be heard from outside. They suddenly wake up and become anxious because, for example, a burglar has crept into the house without making a sound. Incidents likes this have been reported several times. If no sensory signals are present and the body's still requires to sleep, then information must have flowed from an origin that points to another mental level Namely, an unconscious sphere that caused the body to wake even though no sensory information was present. This means that there must have been some extra-corporeal information flowing that caused the body to act in certain situations. Yet, these are not consciously recognizable, not even in retrospect. This suggests to me that human action and thought of every kind is initiated from this unconscious, mental level.

I visited an art gallery some time ago and stood in front of a painting. A man was standing next to me who was also looking at the painting. After a while, I said I love like the expressionist style of this painting, to which he replied, 'But the painting has naturalistic style'. I asked him if his eyes were okay, because the painting quite clearly has an expressionist style. He replied in the negative again and then left the room. Now we could arrange with the painting to be examined scientifically, which would confirm or deny the expressionistic styles of the painting and my statement. But what was this argument really about? The crucial point is that human contact is always about experiencing the character traits of the person in question, in this case that of arrogance, and especially of being right. The painting is merely the means by which the argument can take place. In a progressive argument, you usually use the most logical argument or reasoning to convince the other person that you are right. This may be true from a factual point on view, but in reality the above trait is experienced. Perception (of the human mind) is the noun used to express the action of 'perceiving something'. So perception is divided into a something, into the perceiver, the process of perceiving, and the outcome of what is perceived. To perceive something as true means that what is perceived cannot itself be true, because something initially unknown is seen and interpreted through the individual conception of the human mind. This described something is a constantly changing existence without truth. It exists in its description only through and because of the perceiving human mind out of its current conception of the existence in question.

The process of perception itself is in a constant state of flux, because the moment of perception neither persists nor returns, but changes immediately, that is, without remaining in the moment of a new process of perception based on a slightly different perception and a different human mind that perceives. The realization therefore is that truth cannot be sought after or

discovered because it does not exist. All existence passes away and strives for dissolution. Therefore, the search for truth should be a process that is not about seeking and finding some supposed truth. Again, it comes back to the motives that lie in the nescience and that experience themselves.

What is thinking?

Thinking is usually distinguished from perception and intuition. This is usually justified by the fact that perception and intuition are non-conceptual, whereas thinking is conceptual or propositional. Thinking can be based on a sudden idea, spontaneously triggered by feelings, situations, sensations, or people, or can be developed in an abstract-constructive way. Automatic thinking, which is unconscious, unintentional, involuntary, and effortless, can be distinguished from controlled thinking, which is conscious, intentional, voluntary, and requires effort. How thinking occurs in detail is the subject of research in various disciplines. The sociology of knowledge, ethnology, psychology (especially the psychology of thinking), and cognitive science view thinking in very different ways. Some disciplines try to describe the existing forms of thinking and to find certain patterns and heuristics that individual or groups thinking follow in general, group-specifically or in individual cases. These forms may be viewed from the perspective of sociology, general psychology, personality psychology, or in cognitive science models. Neuroscience and related disciplines study the psychological, neural, and biochemical mechanisms underlying the concrete process of thinking. Epistemology, game theory, logic, and the psychology of reasoning study the rules that thinking must follow in order to meaningfully process perceptions, arrive at true beliefs, or correctly solve problems or draw conclusions.

(Source: Wikipedia)

'We are what we think. Everything we are is created with our thoughts. With our thoughts we create the world.'

(Buddha)

By thinking I mean the process by which the human mind perceives the information stored in the brain. The brain contains information that comes from the physical sense organs, the stored experiences of the past, and the nescience (evil, love). The signals the sense organs receive can cause appropriate reactions, such as fleeing from perceived dangers. Stored experiences allow the human mind to consider its past. Nescient motives transmit calls to action that are controlled by negative character traits on the

hand and love on the other. These are transmitted to the human brain, and thus to the human mind, as thoughts for the purpose of implementing motives. When thinking, the human mind considers the life experiences and sensory information stored in the brain. The human mind can only consider such unconscious calls to action after the action has been carried out. Although there are also thoughts that arise in the brain from within the nescience, the human mind can only recognize them when they are stored in the brain after the action has been carried out, including all spontaneous actions.

Consciousness and unconsciousness - what are they?

In a materialistic worldview, the mystery of consciousness arises from the question of how can consciousness emerge from a particular arrangement and dynamics of matter. Proponents of the view that consciousness is enigmatic argue that even a complete understanding of all physiological brain processes would not be able to answer this question. Many mental states are characterized by a particular kind of experience. For example, the essence of the mental state 'pain' is obviously that it accompanied by a sensation of discomfort. However, the origin of this experience (the pain) remains unclear. There is no evidence from neural or functional states that it is accompanied by an experience of pain.

Often it is formulated as follows: the processes in the brain are (not) yet able to explain why they occur in conjunction with a corresponding experience. Why do so many processes in the brain without a spark of consciousness?

This phenomenon seems puzzling.

(Source: Wikipedia)

Consciousness is generated by the brain; this is the scientifically accepted thesis today. This assumption corresponds to a materialistic view of the world, according to which all processes and phenomena can be traced back to matter and its laws. However, such an assumption is challenged by the knowledge of people who have had near-death experiences. The processes that scientists have studied in patients are all based on medical measurements in connection with cardiac arrest with subsequent loss of all brain activity. After these patients were brought back to life, they reported clearer realities than they had ever experienced in the living world. There was no space or time, and they felt that everything was connected to everything else. Their awareness of other people, other living beings, and the environment had changed greatly, and all they now wanted to do was to work to bring about help and improvement.

In the most famous case, a girl remembered 25 names from a deceased incense seller's circle of friends; who was run over by a truck. She gave the exact names of the brands of incense he sold. These brands were neither known nor available in the are where the girl lived. Such precise information made it possible to identify the merchant. It turned out that he was riding a bicycle to sell incense when he was hit by a truck and killed. The incense brands the girl mentioned were exactly

the same as the ones he had been selling. The girl knew so many details that chance could be ruled out. The details were written down before anyone started investigating the case.
In many cases with such children, birthmarks manifest in locations corresponding to entry and exit wounds on the body of the deceased individual, which caused their death.
Approximately 35% of children experience a concurrent development of a pathological fear concerning the circumstances of the death of the person described in relation their own death, such as a fear of water in the case of drowning.
(Anon.)

Nescience and awareness are mental and spiritual realms that cannot be scientifically proven, described or explained in the same way as physical existences. They are not created by a pattern of matter with a certain dynamic created by the brain; rather, matter and dynamics are arranged in the brain by the nescience according to the information it transmits. The effects of the nescience on physical states and activities can merely be perceived by the human mind. The human mind cannot be physically measured because it has no physical properties; the nescience is the mental sphere that consists of the qualities of evil and the qualities of love, and only in this sphere are all the motives located that lead to observable actions and their effects in the mundane existence, and it is only from this sphere that all human actions are initiated by the human mind and the human brain. No other possibility exists. Consciousness, on the other hand, consists solely of the mental consideration of

sensations, past events, experiences, and ideas about existence stored in the brain. Consciousness differs from the unconscious by the absence of calls to action. There can be no motives in the consciousness because it is the antithesis of nescience. Consciousness, in its pure form, must therefore be actionless. Consciousness is therefore a state of my individual human mind that can theoretically contemplate everything that is in my brain. When I observe what people are doing, how animals are behaving, or how I am moving, I can only become aware of it after it has happened. But if I spontaneously turn my head and see a person walking towards me, that movement of my head can only be initiated by my subconscious mind. No previous event existed in my brain that my human mind could have consciously considered. I could not have seen the person before I turned my head. Therefore, I could not have consciously turned my head. What previous event could I have consciously turned my head toward? When I see that person approaching me, that event is already in the past, and that is the only way my human mind can consciously consider it. The instruction to turn my head before I was able to see the person could only have come from the nescience. So consciousness is not an agent of any action, because consciousness considers what has happened. Consciousness is therefore an actionless sphere that al ways have only an observing character. Every action and every event must therefore have been initiated by the nescience. But a person cannot exist who is only instilled with pure consciousness, because that person cannot perform any actions. Yet the reason for living is to perform actions from the unconscious.

According to my knowledge, the nescience is an unknown divine sphere, or one that belongs to the Creator, and is attributed to both evil and love in its effect. It is the level from which both evil deeds and acts of love are brought into the world. This is particularly evident in the highly malicious actions of people who commit murder or rape. These people cannot consciously recognize their deeds before they are acted out. They act this way because they are unconscious, so their 'mission' comes from their own nescience. Even after the deed has taken place, this character trait can be so strong that these people continue to commit such acts. Acts of love can also be so strong that they cannot be influenced and must be experienced. Nescience manifests itself both mentally in unconscious thoughts and physically in unconscious actions.

Some time ago I was driving back to my apartment from doing some shopping. I was driving down the main road. As I was approaching the intersection with a side street, a car traversed the main road without yielding the right of way; I was just able to brake in time. *'I can't believe it, you stupid cow,'* I swore. As I drove past, she looked at me and raised her hand in apology. After a few seconds I had to smile because, if I had been conscious at that moment, I certainly would not have insulted the lady. I realized what had caused my reaction. It was spontaneous, so it must have come from my nescience. Anger was present in my nescience, and in this near-accident situation, I was able to experience this character trait; I could not prevent it. My reaction came spontaneously and I was unaware of it. I was only able to consider both the woman's action and my reaction after they had happened. The woman

driver's character trait might have been one of ignorance, The was able to experience it in the neat-accident situation, and was impossible for the driver to prevent it. Her action was spontaneous and therefore nescient. She could only raise her hand to apologize once she had become aware of her actions could, indicating that she had no intention of doing what she had done. This must have acted unconsciously otherwise she would have not have apologized afterward. This is how the character traits of evil are experienced. The more evil and love are expressed in this way, the more they weaken, the more the unconscious recedes, and the more consciousness can arise. In other words, consciousness is the conscious recognition of thoughts sent to the brain by the nescience. Becoming conscious is therefore a function of the reduction of the unconscious and cannot be actively brought about. It is always a consequence of the weakening and dissolution of negative character traits and love. Actions therefore always arise out of the nescience because it is the only sphere that possesses negative character traits and the properties of love.

Use Your Brain Correctly! -How to Develop Your Potential – Prof. Dr. Gerald Hüther (Sept. 2022)

At the end of his talk, Professor Hüther posed a question to a team of cyclists he had used as an example, who had quarreled while preparing for a cycling tour:

'Do you want to show the others what smart asses you are?' But they did not want that. *'Then you should treat each other*

differently,' said the professor. The team members put aside their differences and cycled together across the USA. The people in this group found themselves on a mental boundary between the nescience and the conscious, and had already outlived their character traits in the main (perhaps arrogance, self-righteousness). Only due to this were they able to recognize, accept and follow Professor Hüther's call. The weakening and dissolution of evil is only possible once its character traits have been fully experienced. I am not sure know when this might happen, because there seems to be only one direction of information, namely from the subconscious to the human brain, but not the other way round. The assumption by some philosophers that there could be some kind of feedback from the brain to the unconscious, as is inconclusive for me. What sense would that make? Then there would have to be some kind of 'receiving station' in the unconscious, which would then be able to recognize its own unconscious and choose what should be brought into mundane existence. That would require another center where decision-making takes place, and that is not discernible to me. A person who has experienced his destiny, his 'contractual' experi ences, and whose body has reached an appropriate age or is sufficiently deteriorated, will die, unless their destiny is to suffer. Nescience (evil and love) has no need of a body which can certain actions can no longer emanate. Evil can damage to a body through violent character traits, so that it is no longer viable and dies. This can be caused, for example, by a heart attack or brain damage.

I would like to reiterate that a human being is not an independent physical and mental being that makes its own decisions. All actions to be performed come from the various characters in the nescience. They exist in the human brain as thoughts and must be carried out by the human mind. The body is a temporary living system made of matter. It can live only because the nescience exists within it and makes it, the body system, live. This nescience, evil and its antithesis, love, is present in God, is part of Him, for there can be nothing external to the Creator. Everything I have experienced in my life so far, everything I have experienced in the behavior of acquaintances, relatives, colleagues and friends, are parts of both sides, evil and love. There is nothing else. The more the unconscious weakens, the more consciousness comes to the fore. The more consciousness comes to the fore, the less there is to do in life. The less there is to do, the less reason there is to live. The less reason there is to live, the closer one gets to death. So nothing more can happen out of pure awareness. What should consciousness give cause to? There are no motives in it. This does not mean that every person who has passed was conscious. The majority of deaths happen for other reasons, as mentioned previously. In this mundane existence, everything that happens is as it should be, it can be good or bad, but all things needs one another. But as both sides become weaker and weaker in their mutual experience, they will dissolve in the end. Then the reason for life's existence, for the existence of the world and the universe will disappear and everything will dissolve, which also has to happen in terms of duality.

The 7 Negative Character Traits

and their sub-qualities, from which all man's actions in mundane go forth.

1. Pride

(arrogance, vanity, haughtiness, self-righteousness, pride, condescension)

2. Avarice

(excessive frugality, greed)

3. Lust

(hedonism, debauchery, lust, vice)

4. Anger

(rage, retaliation, revenge, fury, irascibility, hatred)

5. Gluttony

(bulimia, revelry, greed, excess and intemperance, selfishness)

6. Envy

(jealousy, envy)

7. Sloth

(laziness, lack of energy, ignorance, cowardice)

Different qualities are always acted out through human beings in mundane existence. This begins in infancy, where greed, envy, and the need for power may manifest.

As we grow older, these traits may become somewhat diminished and new traits such as pride, lust, gluttony, and others may be added. But there is always love, which is expressed in helping others. Love forms the support the other needs to play out their negative character traits.

Morality

With all the people I have encountered or heard and read about, everyone has expected people to do good, to be morally required to do good. Doing evil is judged as wicked, and is rejected and punished. According to recent research, this is the attitude that has ensured more successful survival in the distant history of human development. I can certainly agree with this in my findings. Causally, however, I consider good and evil to be character traits of the nescience, and they do not justify a superior morality that evaluates these character traits as positive or negative. I attribute the rejection and punishment of actions that have been declared bad to the negative character traits of revenge, retaliation, and anger that are present in evil. One of the ways in which they can be played out is by bringing bad, that is, immoral, things into the world and experiencing them. Criminal laws are now used to exercise retribution and revenge, justified by the illegal actions of those to be punished. In my opinion, there cannot be a morality that consists of only the good and condemns and tries to suppress the immoral bad. In a world where evil is played out, there is no moral action, because every action is based merely on the different characters of evil.

Morality itself possess evil characteristics (revenge, retaliation) and therefore cannot be understood as a goal to be pursued above all else. Immoral evil, like moral evil, belongs to the characteristics of evil as a whole and must therefore be brought into mundane existence and experienced. If morality were something good, it would be a part of love and would be incapable do anything bad. Then morality would not be able to call for retaliation and revenge.

Suffering

Suffering is a spiritual expression or feeling caused by physical deficiencies, lack of needs' satisfaction, and acceptance of the consequences of evil actions (character trait of love). A special feature of suffering arises from the different character traits within the nescience of evil itself. For example, the need for power can be counterbalanced by anger and anger can lead to revenge and retaliation. The inferior character suffers in anger because they cannot play out character traits because another character is stronger. Such suffering cannot be part of love, because anger is not a trait of love, but of evil. Suffering can be played out through generations. Thus, physical or mental disorders can even be present an unborn child as inherited traits. These traits are present in the motives of evil.

On the one hand, they are produced by the wicked actions of the parents, and on the other, they are also produced in the developing child in the world without the parents undertaking any wicked actions in connection with procreation. The cause of all human actions is always evil. When a person suffers, the unconscious part

of his love suffers causally. It transfers its suffering to the human mundane mind as a painful sensation and thus plays out its suffering in mundane existence. Suffering therefore occurs even when not physical injury in present. Suffering occurs by permitting and enduring the evil actions of evil, so it is a trait of love.

Guilt

A New Culture of Consciousness with Thomas Metzinger (YouTube video): Every conscious action has an unconscious precursor. Human dignity is generally no longer tenable (globally speaking).

(Professor Thomas Metzinger on free will and guilt)

Human dignity shall be inviolable. To respect and protect it shall be the duty of all state authority.

Every person shall have the right to free development of his personality insofar as he does not violate the rights of others or offend against the constitutional order or the moral law.   (Basic Law for the Federal Republic of Germany)

The violation of basic rights gives rise to guilt.

Guilt is a mental idea that arises from one's own bad actions and their consequences, combined with the perceived personal responsibility for them. Thus, the idea of guilt reflexively leads to realizing that one needs to atone for one's own bad action in order to be punished. Most people believe that every bad deed needs to be punished and atoned for, otherwise there can be no peace.

That is why criminal law was in democracies. Guilt is assigned to those held responsible for actions resulting from negative character traits. Bad deeds are punished. Such punishments also arise from the negative character traits of the nescience. Love cannot be the cause of punishment. It is the very quality that makes it possible for evil to be played out. Love possesses no negative traits in itself. Therefore, repentance can only be justified by negative character traits, because repentance is the cause of suffering. Love made the evil deeds possible in the first place, therefore it cannot repent of them at the same time. Guilt does arise in people who harbor particularly strong motives, such as murderers. The murderer's strong negative character trait does not allow him to admit his guilt. To avoid the consequences of his wicked actions, the murderer uses lies and deception. Even if the consequences in the outside world can be avoided in this way, there are still personal consequences, because the human mind can be so burdened that it becomes sick. This can manifest as psychosis, depression, or another mental illness. It can also result in physical ailments such as a heart attack or a stroke. The wicked deeds of evil, such as another person harming a child, also make it possible to experience other evil character traits, such as revenge and anger on the part of parents. In the evil process itself, love has entered the child's mind and has enabled and allowed evil to perform its work on the child's body and mind. Love itself suffers and endures the suffering and pain in the child. In this regard, I would like to point out once again that all bad actions are caused by the nescience, by evil. Therefore, there are no actions that can be causally

attributed to the mundane human mind, because the mind only translates the negative character traits from the nescience into the mundane existence. Therefore, in the deepest sense, guilt neither exists in man nor in evil, for there is no accuser and no judge of evil.

The Crucifixion of Jesus

The accounts of the crucifixion of Jesus Christ are entirely consistent with the customs and practices of the Romans of that time. Today's celebrated researchers leave no doubt

that Jesus' terrible and painful death is established fact. The only point of contention is the nature and character of the criminal Jesus Christ. Therefore, look at the account for yourself. Despite all his suffering, Jesus thought much more of others than of himself. His first words on the cross were, Father, forgive them, for they know not what they do (Luke 23:34). His thoughts were with of his mother who stood weeping by the cross and He asked His beloved disciple John to take care of her. Two robbers were crucified at the same time, one on each side of Jesus. When one of them recognized Jesus as the Lord, Jesus said to him, Truly I say

to you, today you will be with me in paradise (Luke 23:43). Finally, Jesus expressed His complete surrender to the will of God when He uttered, It is finished (John 19:30) and, Father, into Your hands I commit My spirit! (Luke 23:46).
(Source: allaboutjesuschrist.org)

Gospel of Luke

Luke adds that the sun ceased to shine (Greek: εκλείπειν - ekleipein), referring to the apparent lack of sunlight. Ekleipein is the standard term for an eclipse. The Majority Text, many ancient witnesses, and probably even Origen, pass down the word eskotistä (εσκοτίσΘη): the sun 'was darkened'. Even Luke does not explicitly interpret the darkness beyond this. However, the fact that the power of darkness is at work is already expressed in the Gospel

at Jesus' arrest (Luke 22:53) in His word to the rulers: This is your hour, and the power (exousia) of darkness. The meaning of the double verbal link is obvious. Jesus was thus announcing the visible darkening i advance. By placing the renting of the temple veil next to the darkness (although his sources place the former shortly after Jesus' death), Luke creates an implicit interpretation for both:

just as the darkness rents the day in two, so the (inner) veil of the temple is rent in two. While darkness reigns outside and God's judgment is passed on Jesus, access to God's presence opens up inside. Both have universal significance. The evangelist saw the darkness as 'a cosmic sign' that 'underscores the significance *of the death of the Messiah of Israel' rather than its meaning. According to Luke's idea, it probably extended over the entire inhabited 'earth' (gē) because the evangelist wanted to prove the importance of Jesus for the whole world through his two books, Luke and Acts. In contrast, both Keener and Liefeld understand*

'land' in the local sense to refer to Israel or Judea (as does the Book of Peter, 15).

(Source: Wikipedia)

I consider the description of the crucifixion of Jesus and the various subsequent explanations and interpretations of His death to be correct in their meaning. It is clear to me that this must refer symbolically to the evil that subjugates the world. In the crucifixion itself, and in all the actions and intentions that preceded it, evil is made visible with all its negative character traits. In my opinion, Jesus' statement on the cross, 'It is finished,' refers to the fact that evil and all its negative character traits can now experience that there are no conditions and no limits to evil.

At the same time, just prior to His death, Jesus seems to come to the realization that evil will be dissolved in the end when he says, 'Father, into your hands I commit my spirit!' This means that His spirit must have been in the bondage of nescience as a lover, which, after its dissolution, will dissolve into God Himself.

Death

In the mundane, material realm, death is the withdrawal of the divine spirit from the body. This can happen due to old age, illness, accident, violence, or other causes. Basically, all mundane existence strives for dissolution; it was created that way. Therefore, physical death is the result of this quest for dissolution. It is not the divine spiritual unconsciousness that moves it that dies, but the body created by God with its human spirit. There is no life after death. Since life consists of body, mind, and parts of the nescience, this connection inevitably dissolves with the death of the body.

What is a hero?

Someone who acts with particular courage or distinction on behalf of others or a cause, or who dies in action. - This hero saved his wife and children from their burning house. - In the novella Lenz, the hero struggles to make religious sense of his suffering. - We speak of our fallen war heroes.
(Source: Wikipedia)

A hero is regarded by most people as a good person. A hero protects other people or living beings from suffering, pain, or death. However, in doing so, the hero must also resort to negative character traits and inflict pain on those responsible for causing the suffering, or even kill them, in order to save the lives of others. In the hero's mind, the tension between love and evil is quite apparent clear, and this can bring harm to their body or mind.

What is a human being?

In accordance with my findings, there are two components to the concept of human beings:

The first concept: The mundane, quick human body. The human body is the mundane biochemical, physical, and material system that enables actions, speech, and other forms of communication between living beings, such as between humans and animals.

The second concept: The human spirit that possesses mundane manifestations. It receives unconscious information from an individual nescience on a spiritual level. These manifest in certain mundane actions and behaviors. In addition, there is another equally individual human spiritual quality, that of consciousness, which no longer leads to actions and deeds. When considering human beings, they first of their living, individual body. Other human being cannot perceive more than this mundane physical appearance with their physical senses. However, when we look at each other, speak to each other, and listen to each other, all of which are bodily activities in the first place, other perceptions arise. Affection, aversion, quarrels and conflicts arise, as well as togetherness and mutual support. However, this interpretation of perception can no longer be a physical sensation; the corresponding sense organs are missing. The interpretation of such human relationships therefore have to be created in an individual human mind. As already described above, behaviors and actions only arise when the appropriate information is transferred from the nescience to the human brain, so the aforementioned interpretations must al ready be present in the unconscious. This means, for example, that my reaction to the behavior of other people must come from the nescience because the character-related interpretation is present in it. My human spirit is invariably merely the recipient and executor of calls to action from the nescience. The nescience is the spiritual level from which individual information is introduced into the human brain. It brings its character traits in a combination of both (evil and love) as information into the human brain. The human spirit then causes corresponding physical action via the brain. This is what people do and what is observable in other people. The notion people have of having made the decision to act themselves is therefore not correct in this way. Nevertheless, the notion of possessing one's own free will is already present in the nescience and is transported as information into the human brain. The human mind translates this as thoughts and then lets the body express them as words. Here, too, it becomes clear to me that the notion of man being free in thought and action is actual controlled by the character traits of the nescience. This notion is a spiritual perspective that I attribute to the negative character traits of evil. Thus, it is clear to me that there can be no independent and free human being. A human being consists merely of a human body and a human mind and is the executor in the sense of the nescience.

Human Behavior

In the animal world, killing other living beings is necessary to ensure one's own survival. No one would consider this a crime. Butchers, slaughterhouse workers, and fishermen also kill living things. No law is broken in the process. On the contrary, the keeping and killing of living animals on a mass scale is even supported by government subsidies. Even the mutilation, maiming, and killing of animals for scientific purposes is not only financially subsidized, it is often considered a necessary evil, without whose results humans would suffer or even die. This is in addition to the breeding of animals that have been removed from their natural development and environment. [Other people want to reduce or even prevent suffering and work to reduce and prevent harm through education and offers of help. They criticize factory farming and the merciless slaughter of so-called livestock and call for better controls in slaughterhouses and animal husbandry. But the killing continues. It should only be more humane, with less suffering and pain for the animal. The situation is different when humans endanger, harm, or kill other humans. Then in democracies, the perpetrators are punished with life imprisonment or even death. It is the law created by the unconscious through which negative character traits again such as revenge and retaliation are experienced. I have read about people who thought that people just needed to be enlightened about what is good and what is bad. After which they should be able to see for themselves that they only need to do good to bring about a peaceful world. [However, according to the descriptions I gave above, man cannot be a free and independent being with a self-determined way of life. This is in extreme contradiction to criminal law in democracies. Their jurisdiction is based on the fact that the offender acts freely and without coercion. Although they are base motives, they are self-determined and therefore the offender is responsible for their actions and can be punished. People who are mentally ill and commit crimes while they are ill are also condemned. However, due to their illness, which implies involuntariness, they are not judged to be guilty as allegedly free agents are. They are confined in special forms of accommodation and treated according to their illness. In the case of climate change, I dictatorial rulers do not consider it not important to reduce the carbon emissions of industries and other contributors in their state. These dictators have other things they are destined to accomplish in the world, which they are clearly pursuing. I also see that the pollution of the oceans with plastic or toxins and waste products is far from being reduced or even stopped. The polluters are not able to change or abandon their way of production because their existence or prosperity depends on it. They are not even aware of what they are doing and what they are causing, because their nescience is being played out. I also observe smokers damaging the environment by disposing of their cigarette butts in waterways, on the ground and on roads. For a Brazilian president, the deforestation of his country's rainforests was a matter of personal profit and that of his associates and supporters. It was about their greed, so it had to be experienced. [In the process, many people were harmed as was nature. These are the negative effects of the equally negative character traits of evil.

75

The cessation of greed is predicated on its own experience, and this is only possible through corresponding sacrifices, which are defined as those that are permitted by other people (and nature). How should I explain to a person who has committed murder that their actions are very wrong and should therefore be avoided. Even if I explained this to the murderer, they would still kill people (or other living beings) because in the 'command' to kill has been instilled in their mind by the nescience. The murderer can only act, but they cannot see the meaning of their actions. So I cannot expect people to stop harming themselves, other people, animals, nature and the environment just because the rights appeals have been made to them. The insight into this necessity may become possible when the unconsciousness of these people has been greatly weakened.

Then there is the possibility that only a hint will suffice to make them realize what they have done. This realization and the preceding reduction of the unconscious will not only prevent them from performing such actions in the future, they will no longer harbor them within them. However, because the unconscious is reduced by one's own experiences but does not suddenly disappear, the result of this cannot be absolute and there must be transitions from the unconscious to the conscious. It is also conceivable that the murderer in question is in such a transition and will therefore be influenced by my words. For most people, it is likely that such a reduced level of the nescience has not yet been achieved. I can see this from the patterns of behavior I observe around the world. People can't do anything with the above appeals because their character traits are too strong, and these make them do exactly what they do. In the murderer example above, it is highly unlikely that hardly any of the murderers I wanted to explain their actions to in an attempt to reduce their nescience would be able to comply with my requests. They would be unable to see the meaning of their actions because of the higher power of their nescience. They must bow to their destiny. Reflecting on my youth and middle age, I wish I could return to the past with my present perspective and transform the emotional wounds I have inflicted on others into something positive, such as taking better care of my parents and making their lives easier, or undoing the damage I have inflicted on my own body. However, this is no longer possible, and upon further reflection, the righteousness of my past seems more evident. My personal evolution has largely mitigated my initial inclinations, allowing me to reflect on my past in this way: How could I contribute only in positive way to a world into which I was born, in a world created by God for the sake of evil, evil must be played out. Only when evil can be played out will it cease and dissolve in the end. Therefore, my past actions were bad, but also perfectly right and necessary, because they were brought into my world by evil. And finally, my parents also had to live through their suffering, because that was their purpose, just as it was the purpose of all the other people I had dealings with. This is the case with all people, everyone has their purpose to fulfill. These are destinies, each of which is present in people in different forms, afflicted with evil and/or involving sacrifice.

Love and evil exist in people in different proportions. 100% to 0% is not possible, since neither one side can fulfill all of life, nor is a complete absence of the other side possible. There is nothing perfect in this world. All mundane actions are simply part of the duality created by God. The human body is the system animated by the nescience that allows the characters in the nescience to experience the mundane. This system disappears after the dissolution of all negative character traits. Likewise, the universe, the world, and all material beings created by the Creator for this purpose disappear. Freedom and independence are exclusively attributes of evil given to the evil by God. Evil can do whatever it wants in mundane existence.

Evil is free and independent because it is not restricted by the Creator.

Perfection

Perfection is truth. Truth alone is unchanging and eternal.
The present divine mind is imperfect because it changes.

Imperfection is expressed by the presence of motives, the character traits of evil and love. Perfection develops through the externalization of the motives present in the still imperfect. The motives pass into the mundane body and the mundane mind. The motive is the cause, the creator of life and the mover of the living. The motives are translated and made visible in the actions of the living.

Through the externalization and self-experience of the motives, their weakening and finally their dissolution takes place.

Perfection cannot be created through active action. That would require motives that would cause it. Perfection arises precisely from the absence of any motives. Every being that is constantly changing and the motives associated with it must therefore strive for dissolution. God's perfection arises through the creative mundane externalization of His motives, which are within Him. Nothing can exist outside of God. Therefore, as the owner of His motives (character traits of evil), He must also be the creator of their externalization. Only He could have created the basis for the externalization of His motives by creating the mundane being. Nothing else had to be created, and therefore there is no other reason for the existence of the mundane being (body and human mind). So the mundane human spirit is the divine spirit externalized in the mundane being and afflicted with motives. It expresses itself in each individual physical life with portions of its motives in the human spirit. His motives could not be experienced and would remain within Him solely through the externalization of His motives into mundane existence and the permeation of all life. There must be something in the creation that makes it possible for the motives to act. It is the antithesis to the negative character traits of evil, namely love. Love is the enabling, permitting, and suffering quality of all evil actions. It is love that first makes it possible for evil to experience its motives by providing the corresponding life. Love is the motive of self-sacrifice and acceptance of evil. Thus, to fulfill the needs of evil, a creation has been formed out of mundane being and love. The nature of the perfecting divine spirit is that it cannot rid itself of its motives by a violent act of liberation, for that would again require a motive. His evil motives experience themselves unconditionally through His love. Since the motives of the divine spirit are the reason for the creation of mundane existence, all actions, every experience, thoughts and reflection of every human being can be based only on these motives. There is nothing else in the world. From these considerations came my realization that there can be nothing outside the Creator, because every mundane physical and spiritual being consists of the externalized motives (negative character traits and love) of the Creator Himself. Every human behavior and every thought that has arisen in man reflects the motives of the Creator Himself. In the end, all the motives and character traits that are in God will have been dissolved, and perfection will arise.

The Present Situation

The world we live in today, in the year 2025, is changing drastically and dramatically.

The number of people who are sick is growing, and the number of deaths is increasing worldwide. Not only of humans, but of all living beings. It is estimated that more than one hundred species die irrevocably every day. Overall, the foundations of life and the quality of human life are deteriorating. Scientists have identified tipping points beyond which there is no turning back.

Three examples suffice to illustrate the rate of degradation.

First, the average global temperature of the Earth's atmosphere has already risen by more than 1 degree Celsius, and glaciers and polar ice caps are melting. The resulting darker land surfaces are

accelerating warming because darker surfaces absorb more solar energy. The oceans continue to warm and sea levels rise. Many islands have already been submerged by seawater, making entire regions uninhabitable. The increase in energy in the atmosphere and water is leading to extreme weather events that have already killed thousands of people and caused hundreds of billions of dollars in damage. The melt water from the ice masses also leads to a lower concentration of salt in the oceans, which has a negative impact on marine life and the animals that depend on it. Rising temperatures are exposing large areas of permafrost, which covers about a quarter of the northern hemisphere. This is leading to a massive release of methane, previously trapped in the frozen ground, into the atmosphere, contributing to further warming. New scientific studies point to an intensification of climate change. It is a vicious circle that will soon be unstoppable.

Second, air pollution from transportation, industry, agriculture, home heating (burning fossil fuels), and explosives (e.g., from wars or even New Year's Eve fireworks) is poisoning the air we breathe worldwide. *Studies show that particulate matter pollution alone will cause 6.67 million premature deaths in 2019. The tiny particles, with an average size of just 2.5 micrometers (PM 2.5), can enter the alveoli of the lungs through the air we breathe and* *cause serious damage, including lung and cardiovascular disease. According to the current state of knowledge, there is no safe threshold below which the pollution does not cause damage.*

(Source: Wenhua Yu, Monash University, Melbourne, Australia)

Third, the direct discharge of pollutants into rivers, lakes and the oceans is increasingly poisoning our water. Existing sewage treatment plants are no longer able to remove all the pollutants from waste water. The dumping of waste products (including weapons of war) into the world's waters also leads to further poisoning of the water. Finally, toxins from agriculture and landfills accumulate in the soil and groundwater.

The United Nations estimates that humans dump about 400 million metric tons of pollutants into lakes, rivers, and oceans every year - including thousands of chemicals, nutrients, plastics, toxic heavy metals, pharmaceuticals, cosmetics, pathogens, and much more that may benefit humans but can cause harm when released into the environment. Traces of this constant pollution can now be found in all the regions of the world's oceans - on remote islands and in polar regions, as well as in the deepest ocean trenches. Particularly harmful are those substances that accumulate in the food chain, posing a real threat to both marine life and humans. (see also the United Nations 2022 Sustainability Report)

In addition, political elites deny or fail to understand these man-made negative influences on the living conditions on Earth. Therefore, political policies and laws that would lead to effective improvements are not enacted. In some countries, such politicians are supported by a large number of citizens, which causes incomprehension among other citizens and leads to the formation of opposing camps. In many EU countries, the present governments are being criticized and hard-right parties are gaining support. Furthermore, people who warn of impending disasters seem to have little support from decision-makers with similar views. The suffering and misery of many people will grow significantly in the coming decades. The numerous deaths and the constant spread of disease among humans and other living beings go unnoticed by those responsible. They fail to notice, or they do not care, and if they do notice, they obviously cannot do much about it. Debates in the public media talk about how humanity is behaving badly and how people need to change. But the whole of humanity is not the cause of the global crises; it is at most 20% of all people, if one applies the Pareto principle (Wikipedia). The other 80%, who are not the cause, suffer the effects. On closer inspection, however, these 80% of all people are not only victims, but also have negative character traits themselves. However, the effects of these negative traits are limited in scope and affect only their personal environment. The examples above refer to the effects that human actions have on a global scale. They affect all people and living things on this planet. However, human actions that are confined to a locality, such as crime, mental and physical injury, and ultimately damage to one's own body such as suicide also need to be considered: The WHO, together with the International Association for Suicide Prevention (IASP), has designated September 10 as World Suicide

Prevention Day. In addition to mental disorders, factors such as extreme stress, financial problems, serious illness, and family conflict can contribute to suicidal thoughts.

The WHO estimates that more than 700,000 people around the world commit suicide every year. In Germany, more than 9,000 people took their own lives in 2019. This means that almost three times as many people in Germany are destined to die by suicide than in traffic accidents. In the reality of life, it appears that the majority of people and creatures on this planet are heading towards their end. Can this be prevented or is it inevitable? Can the scientists' appeals change human behavior in any way, and to whom exactly are these appeals addressed? Why do political decision-makers lack the insight to take action? Essentially, all that the urgent warnings meted out by the scientists have led to nothing but political lip service and agreements that hardly anyone keeps to.

Arte.de broadcast: *How does it all end?* broadcast on March 24, 2023

Must everything really end, including the universe itself? Researchers have developed radically different scenarios for the fate of the universe and how and for how long life in the cosmos might continue during these developments. The 'Big Freeze' is one of the scenarios the universe may be heading toward. It occurs when the universe continues to expand and cool, and everything in it continues to decay. But other scenarios are also possible, such as a collapsing universe ('Big Crunch'), or a universe that expands faster and faster and is eventually torn apart by the enormous forces ('Big Rip'). And while many scenarios unfold over unimaginably long periods of time, a sudden end - even tomorrow - cannot be ruled out.

One thing is certain: life on Earth - life as we know it - will have to overcome great hurdles in the future in order to continue to exist. From catastrophes on Earth itself, to a sun that gets hotter and hotter and eventually goes out, to the extinction of all the stars in space and the evaporation of the last black holes. So how long can humanity continue to exist, and what is the probable end of the universe? Can a look at the end of all things open up new perspectives on our own mortality? And: Could things turn out differently in the end?

'Humanity is on the verge of collapse' - We now have twenty years to save humanity from collapse.

But to do so, we must radically change our economic system, our lifestyles, and our values, starting now. We need less economic growth, more taxes, and bans on environmentally destructive behavior. Quotation from the book 'Change'. by Graeme Maxton (Club of Rome)

Humanity and all life will end anyway, not just in the face of the crises described. With the dissolution of our sun and the universe in a few billion years, life will no longer be possible. This is still a long time, but if everything is going to end anyway, what is the point of our efforts to save the world?

This very question makes it clear once again that nothing was created to last forever. The point is that all negative character traits, including fear, can be experienced in this world created by our Creator, and that they will dissolve as they are lived.

Chapter 3

Findings of Various Authors

For thousands of years, many people have struggled with belief in God, with suffering, with evil, and with the very existence of humanity. In the face of global crises, interest in the important questions of humanity is growing, and the search for answers is becoming more urgent. Obviously, no satisfactory answers can be derived from the statements published so far.

In the following, I have compiled a variety of different perspectives from selected authors.

Religionsmonitor, Bertelsmann Foundation

The Bertelsmann Foundation's Religion Monitor 2023 concludes that Christianity is increasingly becoming one spiritual option among many in Germany.

Christian religiosity is increasingly retreating from the churches into the private sphere.

A high proportion of church members currently intend to leave the church. Nevertheless, religion and religiosity continue to shape society.

The proportion of people who believe in God very strongly or fairly strongly today is 38%, and one in four does not believe in God at all. A third of respondents describe themselves as not religious. With each generation, fewer people grow up religious.

Two-thirds of respondents still consider themselves at least slightly to moderately religious, and three-quarters believe in God, even if not very strongly. (Source: Religionsmonitor 2023, Bertelsmann Foundation)

Survey from 2007

Many Germans imagine God either as a person or as something abstract. However, for most Germans, God is most likely a higher power or nature itself. Nearly 40 percent of Germans believe that God works in each person on an individual basis For them, God is an energy that flows through everything, or a law that is eternally valid, or they see him as the highest value.

Almost one in three believe they recognize the divine in themselves.

A minority believes that God must be imagined as an idea without its own existence. However, the existence of evil is one of the greatest obstacles to belief in God; it is probably the most intellectually demanding objection. It is a problem that no theist and no sincere thinker can avoid. The existence of evil is one of the most decisive objections raised by unbelievers against the existence of God.

But it is a Christian belief that evil is used for a higher purpose.
(Source: Bertelsmann Foundation, 2007 survey)

Articles of Faith

According to the Bible, all people are separated from God by original sin.

The New Testament explains that salvation for each individual can only come through faith in God.

Original sin is a term in Christian theology for a state of unholiness that is said to have been brought about by the fall of Adam and Eve, and in which every person has participated since then as a descendant of these first parents. The term is understood differently in the Orthodox, Roman Catholic, and Protestant traditions. Common to all Christian traditions is the doctrine of man's separation from God as a result of original sin. With the help of Jesus Christ, fellowship with God can be restored. Man alone does not have the power to do this. Within the Christian denominations, there are differences regarding the nature of the path to salvation (the doctrine of justification).

*In the **Gospels,** neither Jesus Christ nor the authors of the Gospels speak of the fall of Adam, whose mistake Jesus was to undo. However, there are clear statements about the depravity of the world that can be reconciled with the later doctrine of original sin. (see Bible, John 1:9-11 NRSVACE; John 8:44 NRSVACE).*

The apostle Paul of Tarsus developed a theology of sin and a related anthropology that can be seen as the basis for the later doctrine of original sin. In it, Paul parallels the first man, Adam (the Hebrew word Adam simply means man), who stands for all humanity, with the second Adam, Christ, who stands for the new humanity. Just as humanity was given over to death by the sin of the first, it is saved from that death by the redeeming act of the second:

'Therefore, just as sin came into the world through one man, and death came through sin, and so death spread to all because all have sinned, sin was indeed in the world before the law, but sin is not reckoned when there is no law. Yet death exercised dominion from Adam to Moses, even over those whose sins were not like the transgression of Adam, who is a type of the one who was to come' (Bible, Rom. 5:12-17 NRSVACE).

The central point is emphasized again in Paul's first letter to the Corinthians:

'For as all die in Adam, so all will be made alive in Christ'. Original sin is thus a specifically Christian dogma derived from the concept of salvation, which has no direct doctrinal model in Judaism.

According to Martin Luther and most of the Reformers, man is always already in a state of sin, which negatively influences his own actions from the very beginning. Even the newborn child, according to this understanding, is sinful and therefore in need of redemption.
(Anon.)

The Council of Trent, *at the instigation of the Reformers, finally addressed this issue and declared in the Decretum de Peccato Originali that all human beings in the line of descent from Adam, with the exception of Mary (the mother of Jesus), are affected by original sin. However, original sin is completely erased by baptism. Original sin is therefore, by definition, that defect in man which is already completely overcome by Baptism (or by a corresponding conversion to God, see Baptism of Desire).*

From a Catholic perspective, man incurs God's displeasure through the fall of Adam, since man has lost the supernatural endowment of grace. Without grace, man cannot earn 'supernatural perfection' through his good works. Thus, from the moment of conception in the mother's womb, man is in a state of original sin, which results in man's inclination to evil and the inability of the intellect to recognize good. The senses also no longer behave as the supernatural demands. According to the Catholic Church, original sin is sin in the analogical sense: 'It is a sin received, not committed, a state, not an act.' The way out of original sin is seen in the death on the cross of Jesus Christ and the redemption that comes with it.

Among other things, the Catechism of the Catholic Church states: 'Following on from St. Paul, the Church has always taught that the immense misery which weighs upon man and his inclination to evil and death cannot be understood without a connection with the sin of Adam and the fact that he passed on to us a sin which affects us all from birth and which is the death of the soul' (see Council of Trent: DS 1512).. Because of this certainty of faith, the Church administers baptism for the forgiveness of sins even to infants who have not committed any personal sin. (Source: (Source: Council of Trent: DS 1514).

Joseph Ratzinger does not understand original sin in the sense of a biological inheritance, but emphasizes the collective human entanglements of the past into which every human being is born. This limits self-determination and predetermines the framework of one's freedom:

'No one has the opportunity to start from a perfect zero point and develop their good in complete freedom'. However, in the Catechism of the Catholic Church (Compendium), for which he was responsible, he writes that original sin is transmitted through 'procreation'.

***Islam** has no doctrine of original sin. Although the Quran recalls the Fall (7:19-25; 2:35-39; 20: 117-124) and the expulsion from Paradise (Gen 3:1-24 NRSVACE), it does not adopt the Pauline doctrine of original sin In fact, the Quran (Sura 2, verse 37) explicitly mentions that Allah had already forgiven Adam, which is why the Christian doctrine of original sin stands in contrast to the Islamic doctrine of an all-forgiving God. According to Islamic teaching, each individual is responsible only for his own actions; at the Last Judgment, no one can help or harm another person. If a person sincerely repents of ill deeds before God and asks for forgiveness, it will be granted.*

(Source: Wikipedia

*Neither does **Judaism** have a concept for original sin. Therefore, the expulsion of Adam and Eve from the Garden of Eden is not seen in Judaism as the beginning of an inescapable hereditary sin. The forced expulsion from the Garden of Eden and the subsequent consequences reflect the world as it is and are understood in Judaism as measures that affect the material, but not the spiritual, life of human beings. By devouring the forbidden fruit, however, the instinct of evil* *entered into the human being and has been present in all human beings ever since, influencing their actions. The announcement that the offspring of Eve will crush the head of the offspring of the serpent (Gen 3:15 NRSVACE) is interpreted as a statement about the danger of poisonous snakes and human fear of them (in Christianity, this is interpreted as an announcement of Jesus' victory over Satan).. Neither does the Tanakh refer to the expulsion of Adam and Eve from Paradise in any of the stories in which the people of Israel go astray, because it is not the place that matters, but man's ability to overcome his evil instinct. The most important Jewish statement about the status of the human soul is that it is a spark of God and therefore pure. However, when man sins, he defiles his soul, but through sincere repentance and the consistent decision never to commit those sins again, he has the opportunity to cleanse his soul again, for God is merciful and forgives sins. If Adam and Eve had repented of their sins, God would have forgiven them as well. The sins of the ancestors have no effect on man's soul because he had no involvement in them, and it would be unjust to hold him responsible. However, if he continues the sins of his ancestors with even greater intensity than they did, then these sins are also attributed to him. All of this has nothing to do with place, so there is no direct reference to the Garden of Eden in this regard. Redemption in the Christian sense is not necessary because there is no original sin. Waiting for the Messiah in Judaism has nothing* to do with salvation, but is the sign of the beginning of the world to come, in which all Jews (from the four corners of the earth) will be gathered together.

(Source: Wikipedia)

Redemption

1. Non-Reformed Churches

The non-Reformed churches (Catholic, Orthodox, Oriental) are convinced that the sacraments are the tools without which man can do no good. Therefore, baptism is necessary for salvation. Through the sacraments, man receives divine grace and can attain eternal salvation.

2. Reformed Churches

The Reformed churches (Protestant churches) also believe that baptism is necessary for salvation, but they believe that a personal relationship with God is the only way to salvation. The relationship with God is determined by the portion of God's love that dwells in the person.

3. Judaism

In Judaism, salvation is generally understood as the improvement of the world, or the improvement of God's creation by man, and refers to the 'here and now' in life.

4. Islam

*Islam knows **no original sin in man**. All sins are accumulated by man himself on earth. In Islam, there is hope for forgiveness of sins through God's mercy and willingness to forgive. **A woman cannot** enter paradise alone. She must have served her husband impeccably, and the husband must expressly desire to have his wife in his paradise. In Paradise, the husband is taken care of by righteous women or 'houris,' female creatures who are superior to earthly women in all things.*

5. Buddhism

In Buddhism, human existence (and all existence) is seen fundamentally as suffering. In order to escape suffering, man must engage in Buddhist practice. There is no need for an external savior; rather, man himself is capable of attaining salvation. Thus, when a monk has dissolved all the impurities of his mind (e.g., greed, hatred) within himself, he enters Nirvana after his death and is freed from the cycle of rebirths. In Buddhism, it is not an individual soul that is transferred to the next life, but a karmic potential. The more positive this potential as a result of good deeds, the more beneficial the subsequent existence will be. Human existence is seen as a unique opportunity for salvation.

(Source: Wikipedia)

The Doctrine of Justification

During the Reformation, the doctrine of justification, which Martin Luther considered one of the essential doctrines of the church, became a central point of contention. The Western church had a long history of overlooking or withholding core biblical messages in the name of reform. They replaced these messages with a plethora of traditional guidelines, customs, and regulations. The understanding was that a person could justify himself before God by fulfilling the requirements of confession and practicing piety (acts of love, but also the veneration of relics, indulgences, or masses). Galatians, a central biblical text for the doctrine of justi-fication, was very important to Luther. The churches of the Refor-mation (with reference to Paul and the Church Fathers)remind us that justification, while a very beneficial event for human beings, is entirely on the side of God and not on the side of man. From there, the salvific effect is solely provided, developed and given by Christ. Believers receive it solely through faith that trusts in Him, and not through any action directed toward God ((Rom. 3:28 ESV; 4:25 ESV). Faith, in turn, is brought about solely through the word of Christ's proclamation, which is funda-mentally and sufficiently contained in the Bible and made relevant in preaching.

(Source: Wikipedia)

Luther quotation:

'Thus the human will is placed in the middle like a pack animal. If God sits on it, it wills and goes where God wills... if Satan sits on it, it wills and goes where Satan wills. And it is not in its free choice to run to one of the two riders and seek him...' (Luther, That Free Will Is Nothing. Munich Edition, SV 1, pp. 46-47: see. WE 18, 635, 17ff.)

Joint Declaration on the Doctrine Justification

This is a key document in the ecumenical movement. It expresses the consensus of the Lutheran World Federation, the Roman Catholic Church and the World Methodist Council on the fundamental truths of justification by grace alone. 'Together we confess that human beings are wholly dependent on the saving grace of God for their salvation. The freedom they possess in relation to the people and things of the world is not freedom in relation to salvation. That is, as sinners, they stand under God's judgment and are unable to turn to God for salvation on their own. Justification is by grace alone. We sinners live only by the forgiving love of God, which we can only allow to be given to us. We can in no way merit it, however attenuated, nor can we tie it to preconditions or post-conditions that we must fulfill. The difference between the Protestant and Catholic Churches is still

significant: in preaching and pastoral care, quite different orientations result: the Protestant calls for faith in Jesus Christ, the

Catholic for a sacramental event.'

(Source: Ecumenical Movement)

Is God responsible for evil?

Psalm 13 says, *'How long, O Lord? Will you forget me for ever? How long will you hide your face from me? How long must I bear pain in my soul, and sorrow in my heart all day long? How long shall my enemy be exalted above me?'*

At one point, the Bible goes even further: *'I am the Lord, and there is no other. I make the light and create the darkness; I make good and create evil. I am the LORD who does all these things'.*

(Isaiah 45:7)

(The God of the Bible creates a world in which catastrophes occur that bring great suffering to people. The reformer Martin Luther suffered because God allowed evil to happen. For him, this experience was an almost unbearable contradiction to his belief in a benevolent God. Therefore, Luther distinguished between the hidden face of God, which he perceived as angry, and the friendly face of the merciful God. When he, Luther, was desperate, he fled from the averted face of God to the face of God turned toward him, to Christ.

Without grace, man

According to the testimony of the Bible, man and woman were created directly by God in His image for the glory of God. He was without sin and lived in perfect harmony with God and under God. This relationship was destroyed by the fall of man, which occurred in space and time. The result was spiritual and physical death. Since then, man has lived as a sinner in self-centeredness and rebellion against God. He is an enemy of God in will, understanding, and feeling, in all his inclinations, enslaved to sin in his inmost being, and unable to restore fellowship with God by his own strength He is lost as a result of sin.
(Source: Bible, Matthew 1:27+31; Matthew 3:1-24; Matthew 3:17; Rom. 5:10; Rom. 7:14+24).

Salvation

The need for salvation, for reconciliation with God, is based on man being lost. Its foundation is God's sovereign election of grace (in the sense of predestination) in Christ before the foundation of the world, and the realization of His plan in history in the work of redemption of His Son. The appropriation of salvation takes place through faith in God's promises in His Word, wrought by the Holy Spirit, whereby the sinner is credited with the substitutionary righteousness of Christ, which alone is valid before God. The sinner, thus justified by faith in God's saving act in

Christ, is preserved as God's child on the path of healing by God's saving power. (Source: Bible, Luke 19:10; Ephesians 1:4; Galatians 4:4-5; Romans 8:29-30; Hebrews 12:14; 1 Peter 1:5).

Excerpts from Scientific Research

What is man? Is he free or just a puppet? Science connects freedom with at least two conditions: first, with autonomy, i.e., one's own actions are said to be free if they have taken place without external influence. Second, with authorship, i.e., there must be a distinction from mere chance. Freedom requires a person, a 'self' that determines itself. By self, researchers understand a core of important personality traits and beliefs that characterize a person. Consciousness and the capacity for self-determination are central to the concept of the term person. Our entire legal system is based on the premise that we can be held accountable for our actions. Countless scientists have devoted themselves to the study of free will, but no one has been able to resolve the fundamental paradox: They know that the human will must follow the laws of nature because it is embedded in the physical world. There is no unmoved mover, no one who sets chains of events in motion on their own, without cause. And yet it feels that way. When faced with the question,

'Tea or coffee?' are we really aware that we can choose between one or the other? Or is it just an illusion?

(Anon.)

The Embodied Self-Soul Problem

At the heart of philosophy of the mind is the embodied self-soul problem, which is sometimes also referred to as the body-mind problem. It asks the question of how mental states (or the mind, consciousness, psyche, soul) relate to physical states (or the physical body, the brain, matter, the embodied). Are they two different substances? Or are the mental and the physical ultimately one? These are the central questions of philosophy of mind. But each answer raises many new questions. For example, are we free to think and to will? Could computers also have minds? Can the mind exist without the body? The philosophy of mind has thus become an enormously differentiated project. Plato already addressed this in his dialog with Philebos (30a): 'Socrates: 'Our body, do we not want to say that it has a soul? Protarchos: Obviously we want that. Socrates: But where, dear Protarchos, should he have received it, if not the whole body were also animated, having the same as him and even more excellent in every respect?

(Source: Wikipedia)

Qualia

The subjective experience of mental states is referred to as 'qualia'. But just such a subjective element seems to resist any intersubjective definition. The philosopher Thomas Nagel coined the phrase to define qualia, that it 'feels a certain way' to be in a mental state (what is it like). For example, if a person is cold, this usually has several consequences. For example, different neural

processes take place in the person, and the person will behave in a certain way. But that's not all: 'It also feels a certain way for the person' to be cold. However, Nagel's definition cannot be taken as a general definition. A definition of qualia by the phrase 'feeling a certain way' presupposes that this phrase is already understood. But anyone who does not understand the term subjective experience will not understand the phrase.

(Source: Wikipedia)

Dialectical Materialism

Dialectical materialism uses the method of Hegel's dialectic,, which, along with Ludwig Feuerbach, was probably the most important intellectual source for the young Karl Marx. Hegel assumes that natural and social reality is primarily determined by an absolute idea and develops through (dialectical) contradictions. According to this theory, every realized form of the idea contradicts itself and thus generates an increasingly complex reality. Marx turns the Hegelian dialectic upside down (stands it 'on its head') and postulates that the world, objective reality, can be ex plained in terms of its own material existence and is by no means the realization of a divine, absolute idea or even of human thought, as claimed in idealism.

The theory of dialectical materialism is based on four basic rules:

- *The universe must be seen as a whole*
- *This whole consists of materials that are related to one another, are interdependent, and are in constant motion (objective context)*
- *This movement is ascending, progressing from the simple to the complex, and passes through certain levels, each level corresponding to certain qualitative changes. The respective development of a certain level does not result from harmonious progress, but arises from the conflict and the updating of the respective opposites inherent in the corresponding phenomena, the 'basic contradictions'.*

In addition to these principles, there are three elementary laws of development:

1. *The law of the unity and struggle of opposites (the driving force of development is the contradiction between dual poles, which is fundamentally inherent in natural and social processes and from whose struggle a new solution emerges. Analogously: thesis + antithesis = synthesis).*

2. The law of the negation of negation (the development to a higher level preserves the positive elements of the previous one. In its further development, it does not negate the previous level as a whole).

3. The law governing the transformation of quantity into a new quality (after an accumulation of quantitative changes over a longer period of time, there is a sudden qualitative change)).

(Source: Wikipedia)

Idealism

Idealism (from the Greek ἰδέα 'idea', 'archetype') in philosophy denotes the basic position according to which all of reality can be traced back to determinations of the mind, regardless of whether they are ideas, views, or rather subjective determinations such as 'sensory experiences' or feelings. Philosophical idealism is a theoretical position on the nature of the world (ontology) and knowledge (epistemology).. The term 'idealism' is used semantically in many different ways; in the early 18th century it was distinguished from materialism, realism, and empiricism. It should not be confused with ethical idealism, which is the pursuit of an ethical ideal in relation to society.[2] In everyday language, 'idealism' can also mean an altruistic, selfless attitude. A distinction is usually made between ontological idealism and epistemological idealism. The former is opposed to materialism, which claims that only matter exists. The latter is opposed to naive realism, which claims that the world exists as it appears to us. While ontological idealism historically includes 'objective idealism,' for which the 'objective' world is spiritual (spiritualism) or intellectual (intellectualism) in nature, epistemological idealism represents one of the theses of 'subjective idealism,' for which the world is shaped by our views of it.

(Source: Wikipedia)

Chapter 4

An Appreciation of Different Views

I would now like to take a closer look at some of the statements quoted in Chapter 3, 'Articles of Faith,' to see if and in what ways they share common ground with my findings.

On Chapter 3, Buddhism

In Buddhism, human existence (and all existence) is seen fundamentally as suffering. In order to escape suffering, man must engage in Buddhist practice. There is no need for an external savior; rather, man himself is capable of attaining salvation. Thus, when a monk has dissolved all the impurities of his mind (e.g., greed, hatred) within himself, he enters Nirvana after his death and is freed from the cycle of rebirths. In Buddhism, it is not an individual soul that is transferred to the next life, but a karmic potential. The more positive this potential as a result of good deeds, the more beneficial the subsequent existence will be. Human existence is seen as a unique opportunity for salvation

(Source: Wikipedia)

I can reconcile the idea of a karmic potential with my findings; it is merely another word for evil. In my opinion, living by Buddhist practice cannot be applied to all people. This would mean that all people would have to have the same prerequisites for dissolving the impurity of their minds, regardless of its nature. On the other hand, I know that there are many people who practice Buddhism and believe that they can free themselves from suffering, which obviously has never happened, otherwise there would be evidence of it. Furthermore, I do not see how good deeds in this life can be beneficial to the next generation of human existence. If this were true, who would want to do wicked things? There are no good deeds that could benefit a subsequent human existence. Even parents who have done good deeds in life have children with negative character traits. Furthermore, experience shows that not all children of the same parents are alike in character. Good deeds are associated with evil. There is no good that exists for its own sake. A person lives from a karmic potential. If it has not been dissolved, other people will have to experience it, perhaps in a diminished form. When that karmic potential is dissolved, it no longer exists. Man has no choice in what he has to do. I believe it is true that human existence counts as a unique opportunity for salvation. But in a deeper sense, man is not an independent being, separate from God, but a part of God.

On Chapter 3, Is God Responsible for Evil?

Psalm 13 says, 'How long, O Lord? Will you forget me for ever? How long will you hide your face from me? How long must I bear pain in my soul, and sorrow in my heart all day long? How long shall my enemy be exalted above me?' 'I am the Lord, and there is no other. I make the light and create the darkness; I make good and create evil. I am the LORD who does all these things'. Isaiah 45:7   Line 6 of

Psalm 13 suggests that evil must exist within God Himself. The Bible here explains the dualism of evil and God's love, created by God and placed into mundane existence. Die first lines show the idea that God is separate from man. However, I consider it a fallacy that man is separate from God and is a free, independent, i.e., self-determined being.

On Chapter 3, Man

According to the testimony of the Bible, man and woman were created directly by God in His image for the glory of God. He was without sin and lived in perfect harmony with God and under God. This relationship was destroyed by the fall of man, which occurred in space and time. The result was spiritual and physical death. Since then, man has lived as a sinner in self-centeredness and rebellion against God. He is an enemy of God in will, understanding, and feeling, in all his inclinations, enslaved to sin in his inmost being, and unable to restore fellowship with God by his own strength He is lost as a result of sin.

(Source: Bible text, 1 Matthew 1:27+31; 1 Matthew 3:3-24; 1 Matthew 3:17; Rom. 5:10; Rom. 7:14+24.

The very first sentence makes me wonder why God would have created man and woman for His own glory. How am I to understand that God, of all beings, needs someone for His own glory? Was He bored? The fact that man was without sin and lived in perfect harmony with God, but under Him, that is, in a kind of hierarchy, also raises doubts in my mind. If man created by God was without sin, where did sin come from? This testimony of the Bible seems to me to be an attempt to explain the origin of evil in the world with a 'fall of man that happened in time and space.' However, it does not describe where evil in the form of sin suddenly came from. Again, it is assumed that man is a separate being from God. This leads to contradictions regarding the question of whether there can be anything outside of God. To me it is clear that evil is in God Himself. The arguments for this are presented in this book. The creation of man by God was not for His glory, but physical man was created so that the nescience could experience itself in him and through the human spirit. This is what I see behind this biblical text, including the fall of man. Man cannot have decided for himself that he would succumb to evil, that he would be the enemy of God and live in rebellion against God. He is not in a position to do so because he is not separate from God. Therefore, he is not able to restore fellowship with God on his own, because he is a part of God. Furthermore, in my experience, many people are not only evil, namely '*enemies of God enslaved to sin*,' but they also have a loving and helpful side. For me, man is a spiritual being whose spontaneous mental part is identical with the unconscious. This nescience consists of evil and its antithesis, love. The human being consists of body and mind, but I understand the human body as a tool created by God. The information from the nescience is transmitted to the human brain as commands, which the human being executes as spontaneous actions. Spontaneous actions cannot be considered by the human mind before they are executed.

On Chapter 3, Salvation

The need for salvation, for reconciliation with God, is rooted in man being lost. Its foundation is God's sovereign election of grace (in the sense of predestination) in Christ before the foundation of the world, and the realization of His plan in history in the work of redemption of His Son. The appropriation of salvation takes place through faith in God's promises in His Word, wrought by the Holy Spirit, whereby the sinner is credited with the substitutionary righteousness of Christ, which alone is valid before God. The sinner, thus justified by faith in God's saving act in Christ, is preserved as God's child on the path of healing by God's saving power

(Source: Bible texts, Luke 19:10; Ephesians 1:4; Galatians 4:4-5; Romans 8:29-30; Hebrews 12:14; Peter 1:5).

This passage also presupposes man's separation from God. Through reconciliation with God, two existences would be postulated: man reconciled with God and God. As I have already said, I believe that man cannot be outside God. So the lostness of man mentioned cannot exist, nor can it lead to a reconciliation with God in order to achieve salvation. This view cannot be justified because it would presuppose a separation of man from God. However, it is not man created by God who is causally involved, but the fulfillment of evil and its experience in the world created by God. Man as body and spirit is the means to the end.

I like to cite additional some additional statements by prominent scientists and philosophers.

Kurt Tepperwein: 'You are the creator and everything is possible. Your destiny is in your hands.'

'That is why we are here, that is our purpose: to emerge from unconscious imperfection through conscious imperfection to conscious perfection, that is the goal.'

What does it mean to say that I am the creator and can do anything, including being a criminal? Does that make sense? I would like to reinterpret the statement a little and say that 'you are the creator and anything is possible' probably refers to evil. Because evil is the only power that can do anything wicked, and that without conditions. What do imperfection, nescience, perfection and consciousness mean? Are these states that I possess now, that I will attain in the future, or that I have already attained? How do I

112

recognize these states, and what can or should I do with them once I have recognized them? As I previously explained, man cannot attain perfection because he is not free, not self-determined, and not separate from God. Only the Creator can attain perfection when all evil is dissolved. However, perfection cannot be defined by the Creator as a goal to be achieved by Him, for that would require a motive. Perfection, however, arises from the dissolution of all motives.

Dieter Lange*:*

'Let go! Trust in the basic sense of the universe' 'Disappointment presupposes expectation; whenever you are disappointed, it has only one cause: your expectation, but no one and nothing in the world exists to fulfill our expectations'.

What should I let go of, what should I hold on to? Why should I have basic trust in the universe, and how am I to implement that trust when I am anxious? Everyone lives for and has contact with one or more other people, for this is the only way we can act out the characters in our nescience. It would make no sense to me if each person were alone and completely separate from other people and had no expectations of others. The nescience could not experience and play itself out. The existence of all life and mundane being would be groundless.

Eckehart Tolle:

'If you really knew that you were God and not the little me, you would not react blindly to difficult people or situations, but would remain absolutely awake and conscious. You would immediately accept the situation and become one with it instead of separating yourself from it. Then you would act from a position of alert awareness. What you are-consciousness-would act, not who you think you are-your little ego'.

'This is how you dissolve your ego 'Whenever a habitual no to life becomes a yes, and you allow this moment to be as it is, you dissolve both time and ego'.

How can I know that I am God? How do I recognize it and how do I deal with it? Am I something other than my ego, and what if I am not? What happens when I allow the moment to be as it is? Does this mean that I just look on while a woman is being abused? If I do nothing and feel fine as a result, does it make me I happy? Can I act consciously or are my action determined? Whether I say 'no' or 'yes' to life depends on my fate, my unconscious character traits. I cannot transform anything I do because I cannot determine what I have to do. My thoughts are part of my nescience, and out of my nescience decided what I do and how I behave. The exception would be when my nescience has weakened sufficiently for more consciousness to form. This would give me the opportunity to consider certain evil thoughts. I could then decide not to act badly any more. At least those act that I also recognize as bad that are only weakly present in my mind.

What is happiness?

Many authors have addressed this question including

Sigmund Freud:

'The intention that man should be 'happy' is not included in the plan of Creation.'

Prof. Dr. Hüther:

'Whatever may come, I can handle it - Coherence is when everything fits together, that feeling is happiness.'

Dieter Lange:

'Happiness is a function of accepting what is.'

To understand this, I think about what exactly happiness is and how it manifests itself. I have met people who said they were happy, but they couldn't describe what it was. They were in a cheerful, optimistic, and highly contented state for a short while. They believed it was the result of the actions that they had accomplished and fulfilled. However, I have come to realize that it is not the human mind that creates this feeling of happiness. It is the fulfillment and satisfaction that arises in the unconscious and finds expression in the human mind. The fulfillment of the needs of the unconscious leads to a kind of experience of happiness in God. As a part of God, the human mind is the one that receives and expresses this feeling of happiness in mundane existence.

What is the meaning of life?

Kurt Tepperwein '*You choose the circumstances in which you live.   All of life is a game played for our pleasure. Remove every 'must' from your life, because as soon as you have to do something, the game is over. The purpose of life is to play. Become aware of who is running your life - who is making your decisions? Instead of leading our lives, we often let our mind, and therefore our ego, take the lead'.*

(Kurt Tepperwein, You don't have to do anything! Life is just one big game, inspirer - Discover Yourself) - YouTube 2022)

Prof. Dr. Hüther:

'It is a question of one's inner attitude toward oneself. To experience what it is like to treat oneself with a little more kindness. To live in dignity with oneself. For I am the creator of my own life. To do everything with myself in a way that does me good. To listen to my inner self, to what needs I have buried that really want to be experienced.

For I am someone who can give to others and not someone who always wants to take from others. It is an act of self-liberation'.

Yves Bossart

'One day humanity will die out and the earth will implode into the sun, then we will be part of the past and it will all be over. I have no answer to the question of why all this is happening. I would say: that's probably life, it's just meaningless.'

(SRF Kultur Sternstunden, Does Our Life Have a Meaning? YouTube 2021)

Prof. Scobel

'If meaning is what we make of it, then there is only one answer to the question of meaning, and that is to finally make some-thing of it, and that is something everyone has to do for them-selves.'
(Puzzle: 'The Meaning of Life' - Explained in Philosophical Terms in 5 Simple Steps, YouTube 2021)

Dieter Lange

'Is the meaning of life to be found in one's own contentment or simply by switching off, namely in peace of mind? Yes!' (Taking Time Out: How to Find Meaning in Your Life // Dieter Lange, Greator, YouTube 2018)

It would probably be very nice for many people if life were just a game and we played it for our pleasure. The question of who initi-ated this game for our pleasure remains unanswered. In real life, however, things are different. All people can probably recount that pain and suffering make up a large part of their lives. They cannot really consider these experiences as a game they play for their own pleasure. They were not given a choice whether they have these experiences or not, otherwise they would probably not have chosen pain and suffering. I am convinced that the all life and mundane existence will dissolve in the end, as I have already described. Until then, however, the meaning of it all is that certain actions and behaviors have to be performed. These actions and behaviors form part of our mundane existence. The initiator of every action and behavior is the nescience, which consists of evil and love; there is nothing else. I believe that achieving personal satisfaction in life is a common goal that most people have. But satisfaction is a state of contentment in the nescience. It is expressed in the human mind. This satisfaction in the unconscious comes only after experiencing and fulfilling the motives of the nescience and is dispatched into the mundane existence, into the human mind. I find it interesting that all the authors always describe the positive as what is to be achieved. None of them seem to consider whether experiencing the wicked also has meaning, since wicked things happens all the time. The advice to do only good is supposedly part of a message of love that wishes that wicked deeds are avoided. This is the antithesis to evil and wants to protect life. But good can only be seen in conjunction with evil. Good does not exist in a vacuum. In actions involving negative character traits, love can ultimately only have an 'approving and supporting' effect.

Biblical Quotations

The Lord's Prayer

'Our Father who art in heaven,
Hallowed be thy name.
Thy kingdom come.
Thy will be done,
on earth as it is in heaven.
Give us this day our daily bread.
And forgive us our trespasses,
as we forgive those who have trespassed against us.
And lead us not into temptation,
but deliver us from evil.
For yours is the kingdom and the power
and the glory forever.
Amen.'

Every day, billions of people around the world recite this prayer, either out loud or in silence, always hoping for deliverance from suffering (from evil). This has been going on for centuries, and yet this request has apparently not yet been fulfilled.

The following statement makes it clear what this is all about: '*Thy kingdom come, thy will be done'* can only refer to evil. His kingdom come on earth and His will be done.

'And forgive us our trespasses,' no actual guilt can arise in man, for as a mundane body and mind He is the executive organ of the unconscious. *'But deliver us from evil,'* Deliverance from evil

cannot be brought about by an act of God; evil dissolves through its experience in the world. Another passage in the Bible says, '...replenish the earth, and subdue it'. The statement 'subdue' appears to me to be an invitation to actually subdue the earth by force. The earth is used to experience evil without regard for the consequences. On the other hand, many people understand 'subdue' to mean that the world should be preserved in its entirety and integrity. Nothing should happen that harms life or makes the world a worse place. However, this has not been compatible with mundane reality since the time human beings existed on this planet. In the end, life and nature are being damaged.

Pope Francis wrote an encyclical on the environment back in 2015, stating in a public appearance: 'Our 'home' is being ruined, and this hurts everyone, especially the poorest among us. I therefore appeal to the responsibility that God has given man in creation to cultivate and care for the garden in which he has placed him'.

The statement cannot mean that the term 'subdue' means to do something good. Doing good requires its antithesis, evil. Without evil, no good can be done. So if a man-made apocalypse took place in a few decades, then that is the route that has to be taken. No one can change that. The evil character traits of those responsible must be delivered into mundane experience. As little as I can change the behavior of a murderer by saying, 'Thou shalt not kill,' so little will I be able to change the behavior of those responsible mentioned above. They will change their behavior on their own when they have experienced the corresponding character traits and dissolved them. The reason for creation is precisely that matter and life are destroyed by the evil that occurs in the world. The majority of people and other living beings are destined to have their negative character traits revealed to them. The negative character traits of those responsible for the world's crises need the majority of other people to be able to manifest themselves.

God created all mundane existence in dualism for this purpose, and that is the only thing that makes sense to me.

Conclusion

The statements made by the quoted authors have one thing in common: they talk **about** something specific. They refer to the other people's behavior. They recommend what other people should do to live a better life. They are not talking about the motives that exist within themselves. They do not refer to the motives behind their appeals. How can people accept the appeals that these authors make when wicked actions are present in their minds as thoughts? If someone were in a situation where they were acting out negative character traits, they would not be able to see how the quoted statements would help them. Man cannot act other than as determined by the nescience. That is why man and mundane existence were created by the Creator.

The appeals made by these authors, which are all well-intentioned and designed to help people and halt the deterioration of their living conditions, do not reach those responsible. Similar to a smoker or an alcoholic who damages their body in a way that may put their life in danger, warnings from close family or doctors are ineffective as long as the negative character trait has been insufficiently experienced and weakened. The smoker or alcoholic does not care that his body may become sick or die, because that is not the point. What may happen to one's body, to other living beings, or to the environment is of no importance. Only the experience of evil matters. After all, the nescient mind can create human bodies and other living beings time and time again, and there is enough mundane 'matter' to do so.

Therefore, the evil actions of negative traits and their consequences cannot be stopped until they are sufficiently experienced. Moreover, they cannot all be acted out at the same time. They are too many, too strong and too diverse. In being played out, they will decimate all life, including human life, and limit living conditions. Once this has happened, living conditions must improve before living beings can develop and reproduce again. After all, human bodies and brains are not yet sufficiently developed to be able to experience the last remaining motives in order to be bale to survive. The statements made by the aforementioned authors can help those people who are on the threshold of consciousness. These are people who have already largely weakened or dissolved their personal fate as part of their nescience. Some of them may be helped by the authors' appeals to further reduce their nescience in that they are able to consider and evaluate their thoughts. The statements and appeals of the quoted authors can be taken up by those who are already seeking them. The authors, in turn, need these other people in order to perform their own work. Their work consists of writing down the aforementioned warnings and suggestions, which also come from the nescience. Looking at the world as a whole, however, I can assume from the news and my own experience that most people are still far from having acted out their nescience or having weakened it to a large extent. There in no help for these people, nor can their situation be changed by well-intentioned appeals. Neither will they feel specifically addressed. The appeals of the quoted authors are illustrated in the following situations. A person (body and mind) leads their life, which consists, for example, in exercising power.

They come to a fork in the road where they are called to, 'Take this other path, it is the better one'. How will this appear to them? They may think that is someone is trying to lead them astray. 'I will not allow that to happen,' the person may think. This appeal might rather confirm that the path that they are on is already the right path. When another person with a thirst for power comes to the fork in the road, they may react differently if this character trait has been greatly weakened. They may take the fork in the road because it is their new path in life. It could, for instance, be a new character trait that needs to be experienced.

Someone who is under an enormous amount of stress cannot simply be told to 'relax' and believe that the stress will subside. There is a reason for the stress that a person feels, and it is important for this reason to be within them and not outside of them. Whatever is outside, which seems to create the stress, merely represents the occasion to activate and act out this state in this person's human mind. This makes the appeals and recommendations made by the quoted authors conclusive. They also come from the nescience, and nothing happens without a reason.

To clarify: I am not criticizing the authors or their statements. This forms part of their work and part of their life's purpose, which is generated from the nescience.

It would probably be similar with me. Like some authors, I see my work precisely in making my findings and conclusions public. This also has to be brought out of the nescience through my human mind into mundane existence and experienced.

Chapter 5

Summary and Conclusion

Humanity and all life on our planet are increasingly and seemingly inevitably heading towards a man-made catastrophe. Most scientists have been warning for decades about the dramatic consequences of human impact on the environment. Yet there has been no moderation or even reversal in the behavior of those responsible. More and more people are trying to turn the tide to ensure a future worth living. Worldwide, protests by young people against environmental degradation are on the increase and attracting a great deal of media attention. But the reason for their protests - the destruction of the environment - receives a lot less coverage in the media. Many criticize the actions of these young people and claim that the problem of climate change is not that serious. People point to the fact that Germany is only responsible for around 2% of global carbon emissions pollution. The people and states responsible for inexorably destroying the environment are so caught up in their nescience that they fail to see the impact of their actions. This makes them resistant to criticism. On the one hand, there are people who fear catastrophic conditions in their future lives, and on the other, many people deny or do not acknowledge this. In my own life, I have had to do things that have placed a burden on me and on others. But as a result, this I have gained many insights that have helped me to understand why our behavior as humans is so unchangeable. I have evaluated and questioned many statements made by the Church and in the Bible, as well as the views of philosophers and scientists.

To gain an understanding of my theories, I began my explanations by describing the human body and its mind. I realized that although the body is an independent, self-regulating system, it needs something to keep it alive and in motion. The human mind exists at a mundane mental level connected to the human body. The human mind spontaneously translates the information sent from the unconscious into physical actions enacted by the human body. To the question whether man is free in his decisions, I have to say no. Man is not the original cause of his own physical actions and behavior. The initiative comes from the nescience. The nescience sends information about its character traits to the human brain, which the human mind interprets as thoughts. The human mind translates these thoughts into physical actions. I define the nescience as the sum of the negative character trait of evil and the character trait of love. Love is the character trait that enables, allows and endures evil to experience itself.

Furthermore, I argue that our world and life itself could not have come about by chance. Chance merely characterizes the ignorance of the human mind, which cannot grasp all the conditions that lead to events. Therefore, a creative act by a Creator, whatever He is called, must have taken place, who created temporary existences. The world and life were created because of the evil present in God Himself. There is no other reason for their existence. However, it is a temporary existence that dissolves after experiencing all the evil in this world. When the evil is gone, the creation will also dissolve because the reason for its existence has become obsolete. For me it is conclusive that all life and all material existence is striving for its dissolution. I recognize impermanence and dissolution in every moment I observe the experience of my own existence. Just in the same way that every second, every minute and every hour passes and what I have experienced during this time can never be repeated, so it is with all existence. I have come to the realization that a creation can only be formed in a dual existence. Every being also harbors its antithesis within itself. So everything that exists is subject to impermanence. In the near future, humanity will reduce itself, but it will not perish. In evil, there is still great potential for negative character traits to be experienced. Therefore, the weakened nature and the damaged environment will recover, and the number of living beings will grow again. A kind of new beginning will take place. Finally, I have also come to understand that the world and human life serve only one purpose: to enable evil to play out its negative character traits. That is the destiny and purpose of our lives, and cannot be changed. Mundane and human existence is only temporary. Man is not an independent being, but a part of the divine existence, which has been created. Until the dissolution of life and the world, love and evil are inseparable.

After their dissolution, the Creator will become perfect.

I hope that the contents of my book will help your, the reader, to gain insights that will make your life more understandable and that you can relate to your own life experiences.

I would like to sign off with a quotation from Mark Twain:

'I don't like to commit myself about heaven and hell - you see, I have friends in both places'.

Yours

Werner Loos

Literary References

Wenhua Yu, Monash University, Melbourne, Australia

WWF Germany United Nations Sustainability Report 2022 Animal Society e.V. From the Final Document Synod 2021-2023 Conference of the 12th Synod of the Protestant Church in Germany (EKD), November 8th and 9th, 2020 Climate Bible of the EKD Germany WHO Bertelsmann Foundation, Religionsmonitor 2023 Bertelsmann Foundation, Survey from 2007 Arte.de How does it all end? Broadcast om March 24th, 2023 Biblical Quotations see John 1:9-11 NRSVACE; John 8:44 NRSVACE, Rom. 5:12-17 NRSVACE, see (Source: Council of Trent: DS 1512 and 1514 Quran: Gen. 3:1-24 NRSVACE, 7:19-25; 2:35-39; 20: 117-124 Source: allaboutjesuschrist.org

Source: Wikipedia